S0-BSR-356

IDENTITY

Community, Culture, Difference

IDENTITY

Community,
Culture,
Difference

edited by Jonathan Rutherford

LAWRENCE & WISHART
LONDON

Lawrence & Wishart Limited
99a Wallis Road
London E9 5LN

First published 1990
Reprinted 1998

© Lawrence & Wishart, 1990

Each essay © the author, 1990

This book is sold subject to the condition that it
shall not, by way of trade or otherwise, be lent,
re-sold, hired out or otherwise circulated
without the publisher's prior consent in any
form or binding or cover other than that in
which it is published and without a similar
condition including this condition, being
imposed on the subsequent purchaser.

Photoset in North Wales by
Derek Doyle & Associates, Mold, Clwyd

Contents

A Place Called Home: Identity and the Cultural Politics of Difference

JONATHAN RUTHERFORD

The old forms of existence have worn out, so to speak, and the new ones have not yet appeared and people are prospecting as it were in the desert for new forms.[1]

Saul Bellow

When I began thinking about difference I was drawn to that 'boy's own' fantasy of Lawrence of Arabia. It didn't surprise me when it reappeared, to much critical acclaim, on the big screen. It wasn't just my own feelings of masculine nostalgia that were pulled in its direction. The film and the myth engage with a man who was grappling with contradictory emotions, loyalties and identities. The desert confronted Lawrence with his sexuality, his manliness and his English ethnicity. His identification with the Arabs and their culture displaced the centred position of his identity as a white man. The story is a compelling image of a postmodern world that is challenging so many of our own certainties and our cultural, sexual and political identities.

To the Western European eye, the desert seems an uncanny space, its borders marking out a margin between the habitable and the inhabitable. Yet despite its strangeness it holds a seductive fascination: 'In my case', wrote Lawrence in *The Seven Pillars of Wisdom*, 'the effort for these years to live in the dress of Arabs, and to imitate their mental foundation, quitted me of my English self and let me look at the West and its conventions with new eyes: they destroyed it all for me'. Here lies the desert as a cultural metaphor:

9

in representing the margins of our culture and the knowledge and values that underpin it, it is also the place of their undoing. For Lawrence the desert left him neither Arab nor English: 'I had dropped one form and not taken on another'. In a more contemporary setting Baudrillard has commented, 'in the desert one loses one's identity'.[2]

In the hierarchical language of the West, what is alien represents otherness, the site of difference and the repository of our fears and anxieties. My fascination with Lawrence was that he experienced and expressed the disruptive and unsettling effect of the encounter of the marginal with its centre. The desert as a metaphor of difference speaks of the otherness of race, sex and class, whose presence and politics so deeply divide our society. It is within their polarities of white/black, masculine/feminine, hetero/homosexual, where one term is always dominant and the other subordinate, that our identities are formed. Difference in this context is always perceived as the effect of the other. But a cultural politics that can address difference offers a way of breaking these hierarchies and dismantling this language of polarity and its material structures of inequality and discrimination.

We can use the word difference as a motif for that uprooting of certainty. It represents an experience of change, transformation and hybridity, in vogue because it acts as a focus for all those complementary fears, anxieties, confusions and arguments that accompany change. But as an approach to cultural politics it can help us make sense of what is happening: it can be a jumping-off point for assembling new practices and languages, pulling together a diversity of theories, politics, cultural experiences and identities into new alliances and movements. Such a politics wouldn't need to subsume identities into an underlying totality that assumes their ultimately homogeneous nature. Rather it is a critique of essentialism and mono-culturalism, asserting the unfixed and 'overdetermined' character of identities. The cultural politics of difference recognises both the interdependent and relational nature of identities, their elements of incommensurablity and their political right of autonomy.

'Masochism', wrote Jean-Paul Sartre, 'is characterised as a species of vertigo, vertigo not before the precipice of rock and earth, but before the abyss of the Other's subjectivity'.[3] In Sartre's masculine and ambivalent attitude to masochism lies the centre's characteristic fear of difference – the racial supremacist's fear of pollution and swamping, the homophobe's fear of contamination and homosexual seduction, the masculine taboo of passivity. The centre invests the Other with its terrors. It is the threat of the dissolution of self that ignites the irrational hatred and hostility as the centre struggles to assert and secure its boundaries, that construct self from not-self. In political terms, it has been the Right which has always appealed to this frontier of personal anxiety. At the heart of its hegemonic politics has always been that mobilising of a mass cathexis onto issues of racial, sexual and national politics. The Right (and Thatcherism) always have promised strong defences and well-policed frontiers against the transgressive threat and displacements of difference. Even as it claims the universal nature of its constituent identities, its struggle to maintain the cultural, sexual and racial dichotomies of Self and Other make and reproduce social formations of domination and inequality.

Paradoxically, capital has fallen in love with difference: advertising thrives on selling us things that will enhance our uniqueness and individuality. It's no longer about keeping up with the Joneses, it's about being different from them. From World Music to exotic holidays in Third-World locations, ethnic tv dinners to Peruvian knitted hats, cultural difference *sells*. This is the 'difference' of commodity relations, the particular experience of time and space produced by transnational capital. In the commodification of language and culture, objects and images are torn free of their original referents and their meanings become a spectacle open to almost infinite translation. Difference ceases to threaten, or to signify power relations. Otherness is sought after for its exchange value, its exoticism and the pleasures, thrills and adventures it can offer. The power relation is closer to tourism than imperialism, an expropriation of meaning rather than materials.

Alongside this promotion of difference in the marketplace there have been attempts to reassert traditional moral and sexual values which de-legitimise plurality and diversity, as Western capital tries to assert a disciplined and disciplining society that will reproduce the logic of capitalist production. Since the late 1960s and Heath's

11

Selsdon Man policies of the 1970 general election the Right has mobilised the family and nation as central themes of its hegemonic identity. 'The family and its maintenance', Mrs Thatcher has argued, 'really is the most important thing not only in your personal life but in the life of any community, because this is the unit on which the whole nation is built'.[4] The politics of the family, sexuality and race have contributed to shifting the sites and language of national political discourse: 'pretended families', Aids, immigration, ethnicity and national identity have increasingly replaced the codes of class politics.

Class is still a conceptual necessity for understanding the dynamics of society, but the restructuring of its processes and the decline of old class identities and cultures has coincided with a proliferation and dispersal of *other* political and social antagonisms. Writing from within this interregnum has been a process of relocating myself, both personally and politically. While my politics are marginal to the dominant political discourses of our ailing representative democracy, subjectively I am writing from the centre, within those ideological, discursive and material structures that form the centred (though never complete or stable) sources of power and knowledge. Most writing on the cultural politics of difference has been formulated from marginal positions – those places that my own ethnic, sexual and class location has constructed as the Other. The emergence of feminism, gay liberation and black politics struggled to turn those places from sites of oppression and discrimination into spaces of resistance. In doing so, in asserting the relational nature of identities, they disrupted my own sense of self, revealing the absences, denials and splitting my identity was based on.

Perhaps this explains my fascination with the Lawrence myth and why it works for me as a metaphor of uncertainty. For those of us positioned within the privileged discourses and structures of power, who have crossed those demarcation zones through friendships, love affairs and marriages, or in our political activities and solidarities, that often intimate, unsettling and disruptive relation between the centre and the margin displaces us. In the complex conjunctures of sex, race and class, and the multiple and micro-relations of discrimination and domination, most of us cross these boundaries, both in our individual subjectivities and our personal relationships. Whoever we are, difference threatens to decentre us. In this respect the Right, in its articulation of order and the yearning for familiarity and a sense of belonging, addresses a little part of us all.

Identity and the Left: Two to Tangle

Hey pal! How do I get to town from here?
And he said: Well just take a right where they're going to build that new shopping mall. Go straight past where they're going to put in the freeway and take a left at what's going to be the new sports centre. And keep going until you hit the place where they're thinking of building that drive-in bank. You can't miss it.
And I said: This must be the place.[5]

So the place I am writing from is somewhere in motion. Laurie Anderson's postmodern elegy on loss and displacement speaks to my own uncertainty in writing politics from within a tradition that has held to 'lines' and 'positions'. Lynne Segal, in a critical question in her essay 'Slow Change or No Change: Feminism, Socialism and the Problem of Men',[6] insisted on a response from those of us whose relation to 'the Left' is both in it and against it: 'and where do these new and harsher critics of the Left think they have sprung from anyway?' Her inference is that we have come from a specific libertarian Left that she now sees us as turning on and castigating. But she raises a more complex problem of political identification that cannot be reduced to fixed positions. In the sense of a narrative, my past was in that moment in the 1970s: the 'free school' movement, anti-nuclear politics, men's anti-sexism, anarchism, and later the cultural politics of punk. But I am no longer there and these no longer exist, at least in the forms that I knew them. My relationship to them was primarily symbolic, and so too with the wider 'Left': it was a mapping of my phenomenological experience onto an imaginary homogeneous body. 'The Left' was our term of identification. But the experience of the last ten years suggests that this 'Left' is not simply heterogeneous (we've always known that) but is now so diverse that its constituent parts have no underlying shared logic, values or politics. It is meaningless to talk about 'the

Left' unless it is for purely pragmatic, electoral or tactical reasons –
and barely meaningful then.

Identification, if it is to be productive, can never be with some
static and unchanging object. It is an interchange between self and
structure, a transforming process. If the object remains static,
ossified by tradition or isolated by a radically changing world, if its
theoretical foundations cannot address that change, then its culture
and politics lose their ability to innovate. Its symbolic language can
only conjure up the past, freezing us in another moment. Meaghan
Morris offers an anecdote of just such a body:

> Yet this figure (The Left), mythic as it may well be, in fact defines many
> of my anxieties about politics ... Who could forget Juliet Mitchell's visit
> to Sydney, soon after the publication of *Psychoanalysis and Feminism?*
> ... Mitchell completed a generous and enlightening lecture on her work
> only to be greeted instantly with that voice, that nightmare voice of the
> Left, yelling boldly from up the back of the room, 'Yeah Juliet, what
> about Chile?'[7]

That voice belongs to a 'Left' struggling to hold on to its certainties,
clinging to some imaginary identity like an anxious child to its
departing mother. This oedipal drama resonates with my own
political identification: the 'Left' has been like that pre-oedipal
mother that I at once needed and wanted to move beyond. But this
ambivalence, the simultaneous need for sameness and differentiation ressurects that fear of difference. To return to my earlier
cultural metaphor, that indignant challenge is the voice in the
desert, not simply lost, but confronted by difference and unable to
live with it. So I see this as the place I am leaving, this imaginary
monolith called 'the Left' and my ambivalent identification with it.
My departure begins in the spirit of June Jordan's comment: 'But
everybody needs a home so at least you can have some place to leave
which is where most folks will say you must be coming from.'[8]

In 1983 I joined the Communist Party. Its commitment to
alliances, and the growing influence of a Gramscian politics of
hegemony, introduced me to the contradictory and often fraught
relationship which the more thoughtful parts of the organised Left
had with the politics of difference. During the 1970s the new social
movements had confronted socialism and Marxism with new

political subjects and practices. While they addressed structural and institutional inequality in a language the Left could recognise as its own, their reflexive politics was more than the 'old' and 'new' Lefts and their theoretical constructs could cope with. Western Marxism's emphasis on big pictures, and the practice of 'reading off' the objective relations of class forces, couldn't address these emerging antagonisms. In shifting the parameters of politics to include personal and private life they undermined the Left's narrow conception of equality and exposed Marxism's inability to account for this new politics of the subject. At the same moment that the Left provided the birthplace for new political constituencies, it attempted to deny their difference. A narrowly defined economic materialism that reduced all social relations to the determining presence of class sought to prove the underlying homogeneity of these different identities.

The emergence of a new libertarian 'New Left' offered another position that recognised the autonomous nature of the social movements. Organised around predominantly social issues such as squatting, feminism and sexual politics, it broke with the hierarchical and statist traditions of the organised Left. Affinity groups and consciousness raising, therapy and new forms of personal and sexual morality, were introduced into the conventional context of class politics. But despite its heterogenous nature, the diversity of its activities and its interrelationship with sections of the new social movements, its theoretical base remained within a classical conception of Marxism. This undermined its ability to theorise the different determinations and interrelationships of the new subjects of the social movements. In consequence groups like Big Flame remained committed to a politics that still reduced social antagonisms to a class politics. The belief in some underlying totality that united differences into homogeneity remained.

With the onset of economic recession the libertarian Left died out in the early 1980s. Whatever its failings, it had provided a political space for reappraising Marxism and struggling with the politics of difference, perhaps best exemplified in the *Beyond the Fragments* initiative. It was a process aided by the rediscovery of Gramsci's writings in the early 1970s. This Gramscian moment was partially encapsulated in the British Communist Party's strategy document,

the 1977 version of *The British Road to Socialism*. Its analysis and
strategy was inscribed with the conflicting demands of a Gramscian
'Eurocommunism' and the traditional Marxism-Leninism of the old
Communist International. The broad democratic front was
conceived as a way of recognising the political significance of the
new social movements, and bringing them into alliance with the
labour movement. At the centre of the alliance was the
unproblematised image of an homogeneous working class. The
result was a conception of alliances that could at best be only
pragmatic and instrumental. A transformative politics was
impossible when both class and party were placed outside political
relations. These remained within Marxist-Leninist orthodoxy as
unquestioned certainties, the organising sites of alliances. So was
born that troika of Women, Blacks and Gays, who featured
prominently in the political literature, but whose absence from the
practical business of left politics suggested a deeper malaise in
Marxist praxis. The confusion lay in the assumption that sexuality,
race and gender had no political articulation with class. Their
autonomy was acknowledged, but the consequence of Marxism's
theoretical language and categories was to cast them adrift into the
realm of 'women's issues', the 'gay question' and the 'race problem;'
terms that suggested they were other people's problems, and that
sexism, racism and homophobia belonged somewhere out there. In
rejecting a crude class reductionism, the politics of the broad
democratic alliance couldn't theorise any relationship between these
different constituencies, bar some already determined class
solidarity. The different political practices of the social movements,
and their critique of the Left and the labour movement, were held in
a kind of political quarantine. This failure of theory, combined with a
cultural conservatism, ensured the continuation of a masculinised,
hierarchical and undemocratic structure. With its structure of
democratic centralism and its roots in the era of Fordist mass
production and mass class politics, the CP became as anachronism in
the light of its own political rhetoric and representation.

While the Communist Party struggled to come to terms with a
changing political landscape, sections of the Left within the Labour
Party were attempting to incorporate the new social movements and
their constituencies into the politics of local government. By the

mid-1980s, the dominant political expression of these constituencies had become a form of 'categorical politics' that assumed the undifferentiated nature of each identity. The new forms of municipal socialism, in their innovative relationship to the politics of race, sexuality and gender, faltered on this theoretical weakness. Like the CP's broad democratic alliance, it recognised (although perhaps to a lesser degree) the autonomy but not the interrelationships of these different struggles and politics. It was unable to think through the formation of people and their identities within a number of relationships, for example, race and class, simultaneously. Nor could it cope with the complexities of difference both within and between social movements. As R.W. Connell has remarked: 'In the final analysis, categoricalism can recognise power but deletes from its analysis the element of practical politics: choice, doubt, strategy, planning, error and transformation.'9 Individuals simply piled up any number of categories of oppression – black, gay, working-class, disabled, rather like layers in a cake. There was no sense that a complex interaction between these experiences existed.

Against a background of cuts and diminishing resources, local authorities revamped a Fabian style of politics, dealing with competing claims and administering to those deemed more deserving. In this political *cul de sac* mistrust, moralism, anger and sectarianism grew. The net result was a failure of dialogue. White people were embarrassed about race, men were guilty or circumspect about their gender, and sexuality became an arena across which everyone tiptoed. The authority of someone's politics and the legitimacy of their pronouncements was affirmed by whatever category of oppression they belonged to. Political moralism came to police the boundaries of identities, encouraging uniformity and ensuring intellectual inertia. A new kind of 'workerism' or fundamentalism gained ground, that resonated with that of the 'hard Left' who so assiduously began to cultivate the political allegiance of 'minorities' for their internal Labour Party battles.

The miners' strike of 1984-85 was interpreted as a vindication of those sections of the Left who refuted any revision of their class-based politics. Here, they declared, was the working class both defending and asserting a whole way of life. A form of censorship descended, and with it a left chauvinism that denounced any criticism or suggestion that things might be more complex. Any questioning of priorities, such as the debate over picketing, was met with accusations of class treachery or middle-class defeatism. The period of the strike was dominated by a class politics that claimed a moral truth for itself – its fervour in direct correlation to its declining hold on social and political reality. In this respect the miners' strike represented the last moment of 'the Left'. The political machismo of male syndicalism predominated: it was going to be Saltley Gate all over again. Failing that everyone would go down together. Those parts of the Left that retained some critical faculty and a sense of strategy were silenced, sandwiched between the right wing of the Labour Party and the moral tyranny of left chauvinism.

Nowhere was this more in evidence than in the left chauvinist response to the emergence of the Women Against Pit Closures Movement. The women's groups were used to denounce feminism as an irrelevent bourgois politics. Consequently the male-dominated Left felt able to continue its style and practice so ensuring the political subordination of the new political forms that were emerging as the strike progressed.

New alliances were developing with minority communities, gay and lesbian groups, community organisations and feminist politics, that challenged the leftist assertion that the strike was an homogeneous working class engaged in a singular struggle. In reflecting the heterogeneous differences within society, these new alliances represented the kernel of a new radical collectivism. It is worth noting that images and representations of women were a part of the leftist discourse of the strike, but the political contribution of women, the sense that they represented something more than a politics of class solidarity with the men, remained marginal. Women became a symbolic motif of the strike, cheered for their courage and resilience but still subordinated through the denial of sexual difference and the relevance of feminist politics.

In contrast to left chauvinism, the strike produced new revolutionary forms of politics around class and subjectivity. It was in the changing relationships between men and women, black and white, hetero- and homosexual that a new conception of class was being made. The everyday life of the strike produced a reflexive politics that held the traces of new collective identities. In the articulation of new alliances, the identities and the social relations that originally constituted them were transformed, transgressing the boundaries of category politics. It was just such political identities that Gramsci wrote would become 'the first representatives of the new historic phase', 'the nucleus of a new ideological and theoretical complex. What was previously secondary and subordinate, even incidental, is now taken to be primary'.[10]

Gramsci's comment underpins the cultural politics of difference, for it asserts the politically negotiable and incomplete character of identity and social formations. In many interpretations of Marxism, even in its most liberal moments, there is an assumption of a direct correspondence between the economic base and the superstructure. Class is considered as an 'always-already' determined factor whose constituents just need to be brought to recognise their objective conditions. But the making of political identities and identifications cannot be reduced to such a singular and predictable logic. Where the CP's broad democratic alliance failed and municipal socialism's engagement with the new social movements went wrong was in the assumption that these new political identities were fixed categories.

What the political alliances of the miners' strike demonstrated was that identity is not reducible to the single logic of class. It is constituted out of different elements of experience and subjective position, but in their articulation they become something more than just the sum of their original elements. For example our class subjectivities do not simply co-exist alongside our gender. Rather our class is gendered and our gender is classed. This process of the combining of elements into a 'third term' has been called articulation.[11]

Difference: Beyond the Two-Step

Gramsci described this articulation as 'the starting point of critical elaboration': it is the consciousness of what one really is, and in 'knowing thyself' as a product of the historical process to date which has deposited an infinity of traces, without leaving an inventory'.[12] Identity marks the conjuncture of our past with the social, cultural and economic relations we live within. 'Each individual is the synthesis not only of existing relations but of the history of these relations. He is a précis of the past.'[13] Making our identities can only be understood within the context of this articulation, in the intersection of our everyday lives with the economic and political relations of subordination and domination. There is no final deciding logic that masters and determines this complex structuring of identity. In contradistinction to Althusser's famous pronouncement that it is 'His Majesty the Economy' that determines in the final instance,[14] it would make more sense to suggest that its presence is felt in the first instance, setting the conditions of articulation, but in no way determining their outcome.[15] To paraphrase Marx, people make history, but not in conditions of our own choosing.

This politics of articulation eschews all forms of fixity and essentialism; social, political and class formations do not exist *a priori*, they are a product of articulation. Stuart Hall has termed this the politics of 'no necessary or essential correspondence of anything with anything'[16] and it marks a significant break with a Marxism that has assumed an underlying totality to social relations. The displacement of Marxism's universalist presumptions and its claim to a theory of social totality takes us into new theoretical spaces. This 'deconstructing' of Marxism is not intended to dispense with its categories of class and labour/capital conflict, but to refute its privileging of certain inviolable terms:

> Is it not the case that in scaling down the pretensions and the area of validity of Marxist theory, we are breaking with something deeply inherent in that theory: namely its monist aspiration to capture with its categories the essence or underlying meaning of history?[17]

Laclau and Mouffe answer their rhetorical question in the affirmative.

The emergence of a cultural politics of difference is a response to the new political subjects and cultural identities, but also to the leftist politics that have dominated British socialism. In making sense of identity and difference it has been the post-structuralist writings of Jacques Derrida (and others) that has helped to make sense of the absences in Marxist theory. The dismantling of essentialism and class reductionism allows the proliferation of the sites of potential political antagonism, breaking the narrow theoretical parameters of socialist politics. Any social relation, any subjectivity, in whatever sphere of life, is a potential site of political antagonism. Such a politics no longer simply confronts the singular struggle of capital and labour, instead it holds the potential of being a counterculture, able to address the proliferation and dispersal of contemporary social and political antagonisms. Acknowledging the autonomy of social movements and cultural identities, but recognising their interdependent nature opens up the space for individual historical agency. Our human intentions are neither displaced to some other level, nor are they 'always-already' present, rather they are the product of a complex matrix of different elements. In 'The Relation of the Poet to Daydreaming', Freud captured this process of intention when he talked about wishes:

> You will see from such an example how the wish employs some event in the present to plan a future on the pattern of the past.[18]

In spite of Derrida's diffidence about politics and his refusal to engage with Marxism, his writing provides a language to theorise difference. As a philosopher he has attempted to deconstruct the way in which Western systems of knowledge rely upon some originating moment of truth or immanence, from which our whole hierarchy of meaning springs. This dependence upon a guarantee of meaning that transcends signification is termed logocentrism. By invoking its claim to universal truth, such a system of knowledge hides cultural diversity and conceals the power structures that preserve the hierarchical relations of difference. Central to this logocentric form of thinking is a system of binary operations and distinctions. Those terms that are pre-eminent and invested with truth, achieve that status by excluding and marginalising what they are not. A good example of this binarism is the construction of sexual difference that pervades our language. Active/passive, culture/ nature, rational/emotional, hard/soft, masculine/feminine, these dichotomies are inscribed with gendered meaning: they are the products of historical and ideological forces that underpin and legitimise women's subordination and oppression.

One term, in its discursive and material operation, represents the centre; the excluded term is the margin. By assembling the heterogeneous possibilities of meaning within language into fixed dichotomies, binarism reduces the potential of difference into polar opposites. This stasis of meaning, regulates and disciplines the emergence of new identities. It is at this point, where the potentialities of meaning are congealed into fixity that the margin is established. But it is more than a simple boundary marking the outer limits of the centred term because it functions as a supplement, marking what the centre lacks but also what it needs in order to define fully and confirm its identity. It is then an integral though displaced part of the centre, defining it even in its non-identity.

Binarism operates in the same way as splitting and projection: the centre expels its anxieties, contradictions and irrationalities onto the subordinate term, filling it with the antithesis of its own identity; the Other, in its very alienness, simply mirrors and represents what is deeply familiar to the centre, but projected outside of itself. It is in these processes and representations of marginality that the violence, antagonisms and aversions which are at the core of the dominant discourses and identities become manifest – racism, homophobia, misogyny and class contempt are the products of this frontier. But it is in its nature as a supplement to the centre that the margin is also a place of resistance. The assertion of its existence threatens to deconstruct those forms of knowledge that constitute the subjectivities, discourses and institutions of the dominant, hegemonic formations. It is here, where power relations and historical forces have organised meaning into polar opposites that language becomes a site of struggle. Even as difference is pathologised and refused legitimacy, new terms and new identities are produced on the margins. Those early assertions 'Black is Beautiful', 'Sisterhood is Powerful' and 'Gay Pride' break the logic of the otherness of binarism.

It is this location where identities are made that Raymond Williams addresses in 'Structures of Feeling'.[19] He describes the emerging identities of new social groups and subjectivities as being confronted by a dominant culture whose discourses and language do not allow them to articulate fully their experience. He describes this struggle for a voice as being 'at the very edge of semantic availability'[20] Those necessary words that will represent us both to ourselves and others are not quite in our grasp. The structure of feeling is caught between experience and language, described by Peter Middleton as 'a state of unfinished social relations that have not yet found the terms for their own reflexive self-comprehension.'[21] Williams not only places language within the historical processes of social relationships, he places signification in relation to people's emotions, needs and feelings. In the gendered nature of the theoretical discourses we've inherited, emotion has always been subordinate to rationality. Williams confronts this polarity by insisting that emotions are cognitive: 'we are talking about ... not feeling against thought, but thought as felt and feeling as thought'.[22]

'Structures of Feeling' enables us to move beyond some discrete linguistic realm and so fully address subjectivity and the making of identity. However, this structuring of feeling through language (and vice versa) is itself a gendered process, for the availability of language and its connection to experience is different for boys and girls as they negotiate the complexities of the oedipus complex and their separation from their 'primary love object'. Sexual difference plays a crucial role in the relation of our emotions to language, and by turning to theories in psychoanalysis we can begin to unravel the intense feelings that are structured through the cultural definition of difference. A cultural politics needs to address the many locations created by the experience of subordination – men's violence against women, racism, homophobia, the oppression and abuse of children, class supremacy and so on. These deep structures of prejudice, contempt and aversion characterise the response of the centre to the marginal. A reflexive politics will help make sense of ourselves, the formation of our cultural-political identities, and how they are mapped onto wider symbolic and political identifications.

Today this reflexive politics of difference places us in an interregnum. We are caught between the decline of old political identifications and the new identities that are in the process of becoming or yet to be born. Like Laurie Anderson's 'urbanscape' in her song 'Big Science' the imaginary traces of the future are present, but as yet they have no representation or substance. The cutting edge of new politics and new subjectivities exists within this relation of marginality. But the paradox is that when the margin resists and discovers its own words, it not only decentres the dominant discourses and identities that have suppressed it, but also transforms its own meaning. Just as it invades the centre with its own difference, so it too is opened up to its internal differences. The experience of the women's movement in the late 1970s and early 1980s is a case in point. Lesbian, black and working-class feminist politics confronted feminism with their differential natures. Feminism had to recognise its *feminisms*. Identity then is never a static location, it contains traces of its past and what it is to become. It is contingent, a provisional full stop in the play of differences and the narrative of our own lives. But such an understanding, while recognising the change and displacement of identities must also address the non-discursive factors of class formation and the logic of capital which play a powerful restraining role in determining where and how far anyone moves.

Home is Where we Speak From

Modern life ascribes to us a multiplicity of subject positions and potential identities which hold the prospects for historically unparalleled human development, but they also represent a predicament that threatens fragmentation and psychosis – terrifying in their lack of personal, collective and moral boundaries. In this postmodern, 'wide-open' world our bodies are bereft of those spatial and temporal co-ordinates essential for historicity, for a consciousness of our own collective and personal past. 'Not belonging', a sense of unreality, isolation and being fundamentally 'out of touch' with the world become endemic in such a culture. The rent in our relation to the exterior world is matched by a disruption in our relation to our selves. Our struggles for identity and a sense of personal coherence and intelligibility are centred on this threshold between interior and exterior, between self and other.

If we cannot establish that sense of selfhood, only retreat and entrenchment are the viable alternatives to a schizophrenic and disturbed existence. Only when we achieve a sense of personal integrity can we represent ourselves and be recognised – this is home, this is belonging. Eartha Kitt, being interviewed on BBC Radio 4 by Anthony Clare, recounted her desperate historical predicament of being confronted by white racism and the rejection of the black community she grew up in; in response Clare asked her where her home was. 'Home is within me', she replied.[23] This brings me back full circle to this writing as an attempt to locate myself, both politically and personally at a time when so many people have a feeling of being lost and unsure. My identification with that symbolic Left has always been a search for that most elusive of feelings, a sense of belonging. It was characterised by the belief that somewhere, some place already existed for me – all I had to do was find it. But there are no ready-made identities or categories that we can unproblematically slip into.

For T.E. Lawrence the answer to his indeterminacy was a retreat into the anonymity and discipline of life in the RAF. Perhaps the postmodern world offers us more possibilities. In this struggle for new ways of living, more democratic relationships and new subjectivities there can be no homecoming. Such a politics must be the discovery and making of 'home' – the formation of values and collectivities that move beyond the postmodern and its fragmentation of the social. And I use the word 'home' here, not only as the making of a sense of self and identity, but as a motif for a culture that values difference and thrives on its own diversity. The task of a cultural politics of difference must be to confront a civil society that is fragmented and turned against itself, poisoned by a class system that destroys human autonomy and creativity. We need something more than the Labour Party's call for 'caring values' which suggest an acceptance rather than a transformation of social relationships. A culture of healing and reparation is called for, for the violence, oppression and personal humiliation in our society is such that nothing less will do. The less power individuals have, the more they are marginalised, the more nomadic personal existence seems. In the contemporary context, children perhaps suffer the most, often at the hands of their parents, and in the face of inequality and discrimination our culture tends to turn a blank wall of incomprehension to their pain, humiliation and shame.

Concluding, I have in mind a television image of the 'Women Against Fundamentalism' protesting against the anti-Rushdie march in London (May 1989). Attacked by white racists and some muslim men, they were precipitated into a state of 'in-betweenness', belonging neither in one place nor the other. It is only through their personal, political struggles that they will resolve this indeterminate state of hybridity. By creating new identities they will articulate a new conjuncture in the politics of race and gender. Their predicament, indeed the Rushdie affair itself, suggests that there can be 'incommensurable' element in difference. But cultures and identities can never be wholly separate, homogeneous entities; instead the interrelationships of differences are marked by translation and negotiation. The cultural politics of difference means living with incommensurability through new ethical and democratic frameworks, within a culture that both recognises difference and is committed to resolving its antagonisms. This means a culture and individual sensibility that pays attention to that old liberal adage that we must learn to live together – not attempting to construct oppositions based on hierarchies of value and power, not through that politics of polarity, but in the recognition of the otherness of ourselves, through the transformation of relations of subordination and discrimination.

Notes

[1] Saul Bellow, in conversation with Michael Ignatieff and Martin Amis, *Voices: Modernity and its Discontents*, Spokesman/Hobo Press, London 1987.

[2] Jean Baudrillard, quoted in 'The Politics of Seduction', an interview with Suzanne Moore and Stephen Johnstone, *Marxism Today*, January 1989.

[3] Jean-Paul Sartre, *Being and Nothingness*, Methuen, London 1972, p138.

[4] Margaret Thatcher, interviewed by Julie Cockroft, *Daily Mail*, 4 May 1989.

[5] Laurie Anderson, 'Big Science', from her album *Big Science*, Warner Brothers 1982.

[6] Lynne Segal, 'Slow Change or No Change: Feminism, Socialism and the Problem of Men', in *Feminist Review*, (The Past Before Us – Twenty Years of Feminism issue), Routledge, London 1989.

[7] Meaghan Morris, 'Politics Now', in *The Pirate's Fiancée: Feminism. Reading. Postmodernism*, Verso, London 1988.

[8] June Jordan, 'Living Room' in *Notes Towards Home*, Thunders Mouth Press (USA) 1985.

[9] R.W. Connell, *Gender and Power*, Polity Press, Cambridge 1987.

[10] Antonio Gramsci, *Selections from Prison Notebooks* (trans. Quintin Hoare and Geoffrey N. Smith), Lawrence & Wishart, London 1971, p195.

[11] Ernesto Laclau and Chantal Mouffe, 'Beyond the Positivity of the Social: Antagonisms and Hegemony', in *Hegemony and Socialist Strategy*, Verso, London 1989.

[12] Antonio Gramsci, 'Notes for an Introduction and Approach to the Study of

Philosophy and the History of Culture', David Forgacs (ed.), *A Gramsci Reader*, Lawrence & Wishart, London 1988, p326.
[13]*Ibid.*
[14]Louis Althusser, 'Contradiction and Overdetermination', in *Lenin and Philosophy*, NLB/Verso, London 1971.
[15]This point was made by Stuart Hall in his talk at *Marxism Today's* '68 Show event held at the London School of Economics in May 1988.
[16]Stuart Hall, 'Minimal Selves', in ICA Document 6 on *Identity*, London 1987.
[17]Ernesto Laclau and Chantal Mouffe, 'Introduction', in *Hegemony and Socialist Strategy*, Verso, London 1989.
[18]Sigmund Freud, 'Creative Writers and Daydreaming', in *Art and Literature*, Vol. 14, Pelican, London 1987.
[19]Raymond Williams, 'Structures of Feeling,' in *Marxism and Literature*, Oxford University Press, Oxford 1977.
[20]*Ibid.*
[21]Peter Middleton, 'Why Structure Feeling,' *News from Nowhere* ('Raymond Williams: Third Generation'), No.6, Oxford, Spring 1989.
[22]Raymond Williams, *op.cit.*
[23]'In the Psychiatrist's Chair', BBC Radio 4, 26 July 1989.

Feminism: Dead or Alive?

ANDREA STUART

A recent article in *Cosmopolitan*, 'If Feminism is Finished Where do we go From Here',[1] summed up many women's profoundly ambivalent attitude towards feminism. On the one hand, whether we acknowledge it or not, most of us have a great deal invested in feminist dreams about female autonomy and independence. On the other hand, we also feel that Feminism, with a capital 'F', is unresponsive or simply irrelevant to our needs and lifestyles.

Why is this? After a decade in which women still did not receive equal pay for equal work; in which women were still struggling for control of their reproductive rights; in which women still, by virtue of their sex, in almost all societies and in almost all cultures, fell to the bottom of social arrangements – how can feminism be over? Dead? Passé?

The answer isn't that women don't care about these issues anymore. A recent MORI poll quoted in the same *Cosmo* article said that 52 per cent of women between the ages of sixteen and thirty support legal abortion on demand; 79 per cent of the same women supported the right of girls under sixteen to have access to contraception even without parental consent. Yet, of these same women, who manifestly care about and have opinions on issues concerning women's rights, over 50 per cent believe that Feminism has done little or nothing to help women. So why – when it is patently clear that women still feel strongly about 'feminist' issues and in a new decade where most of the social problems that prompted the rise of Feminism in the early 1970s still remain with us – do many ordinary women feel that Feminism has nothing to do with them? Did women lose Feminism or did Feminism lose us?

This is not intended as a tired, nostalgic lament for the days when we were all girls together in the rosy, utopian, feminist garden. As a youngish black woman I'm only too aware of the battles that black women had trying to find a space in Feminism, just as I'm aware of the problems that younger women have had in finding a voice. So that 'garden', if it ever existed, never existed for me. What I do miss is the positive sense of agency, of being able to respond and change situations, which some sort of collective feminist activism gives us.

So even if Feminism with a capital F (with a lot of help from media depictions of bra-burning, dungaree-clad harridans) has been responsible for losing us, can we afford to lose feminism? Or rather, can we afford to jettison that activist aspect of feminism, which centres around the crucial issues that affect our capacity to lead independent and fulfilled lives? If it were the case that the problems women shared no longer existed, no doubt we'd all be happy to consign Feminism to history – after all it was part of the feminist dream to make feminist agitation unnecessary. There isn't one of us who doesn't want to 'have it all': personally, I'd love to be a 'post-feminist woman' if the problems women face were 'post' too.

Meanwhile back on planet earth ... though women still share many of the same old problems, the gulf between those self-consciously politicised women who describe themselves as Feminists and the majority, often equally aware and political, seems to have widened into a yawning chasm. This polarisation of feminism into the 'professional' and the 'popular' has become the overriding feature of the current impasse. Professional feminism, Feminism with a capital F, seems to have become associated almost exclusively with the likes of *Spare Rib*, Women's Studies courses at universities and polytechnics, and the almost extinct women's units – a legacy of the now defunct GLC.

The work of the academy in particular has been essential both in legitimating women's perspectives and in transforming the way all of us see the world. However, in an age where specialists within any given field are so specialised that they find it difficult to talk to each other (let alone those outside), the professionalisation of Feminism does present problems. Increasingly women have found that they don't have a common language with which to debate their problems and concerns. It is no wonder that 'ordinary' women, those who have not chosen to make feminism their career, feel increasingly isolated from Feminism and inhibited by its exclusivity. To many women looking on at this new breed of 'femocrat', entrenched largely in the middle classes alongside her professionally qualified and executive sisters, feminism seems to have been simply a tool with which a particular group of women engineered their professional success.

Where Does Your Feminism Come From?

Popular feminism, on the other hand, the errant daughter of capital F Feminism, is all around us. It has everything to do with our day-to-day lives. We hear it on the radio, read it in the newspapers, and watch it on TV. Though it significantly does not name itself 'Feminist' it is precisely here (through the media) that the vast majority of women learn their feminism. Feminism comes at most of us through the media, mainstream or alternative, in a multiplicity of guises – as Sheila Grant's traumatic relationships in Brookside; as the independent women conquering Europe in the latest Fiat ad; in a film like *The Accused*; through a BBC2 TV serialisation like Jeanette Winterson's *Oranges Are Not The Only Fruit*, and in popular fiction from feminist lists like Pandora, or the 'women's' lists of mainstream publishers.

Debates around feminism and popular culture have raged constantly over the last decade, not least because feminism's emphasis on the politics of 'everyday life' lends itself to appropriation by the mainstream. Nowhere is this argument more pertinent than in the context of women's magazines: a 'woman-only space' before women-only spaces were invented, they have been a barometer of the extent to which feminist ideas have been adapted and appropriated for popular feminism. They reflect the appeal of popular feminism as well as its limitations.

From *Woman's Own* and its 1986 Rape Survey, to *Company's* 1989 Women's Safety Campaign, what is clear is that across the spectrum feminism *sells*. We have only to look at *Cosmo*, the blockbuster of all women's mags, to realise just how attractive *and* lucrative feminist ideas can be. *Cosmo*'s been selling back to us a common-sense version of feminism for years. But it is *Elle* magazine which has most accurately reflected the postmodern *zeitgeist* – *Elle* in the 1980s was truly a sign of the times. Though it was not *universally* read, it was both radical and instinctively in tune with those times, in its recognition of how key issues like pleasure, consumerism and most importantly the exploration of cultural diversity had transformed what it was to be modern, to be liberated, to be the New Woman.

Unlike that workshop turned self-improvement manual, *Cosmo*, which constantly gave you advice on how to find a man, have an orgasm, get a job, *Elle* was not filled with huge quantities of self-helping advice; in fact there was virtually none. The assumption is that if you're an *Elle* girl you are already improved. Instead of reassuring us that we were all the same, with the same problems, *Elle* stressed difference. It recognised that feminist assumptions about automatic connections between women are pretty hard to swallow. *Elle* captured our imagination because it sold us not conformity but uniqueness, not a cosy experience of universality but a tantalising encounter with otherness.

While Feminism, was worrying about concepts like 'fragmentation' and 'identity', *Elle*, under Sally Brampton's editorial guidance in the 1980s, was playing with them. For *Elle* the image was all, or almost all; words came a definite second. In a world where the only certainty was uncertainty *Elle*'s faith was in the surface alone. No other woman's mag in the 1980s understood as well as *Elle* the compelling power of eclecticism – the *Elle* reader could endlessly reinvent herself being a little bit of this and a little bit of that. Rejecting the coherence of uniform identity, *Elle* was determined to disturb: models were androgynous or parodies of femininity, racially varied and sexually amorphous. Our unpleasant confusions about our identities (what it means to be black or white, gay or straight, male or female) melted into a pleasurable, seductive ambiguity. Through the play of difference, the new New Woman (every decade seems to have one) defined her newness by her different attitudes to pleasure. After the dour censoriousness of the past generation of feminists, *everything* about *Elle* was voluptuous. True to its implicit, post-modern philosophy there was no hierarchy – the pictures of food were just as sexy as pictures of celebrities or the pictures of Guatemala.

Elle tapped into a new generation's attitudes and expectations, with which the feminist establishment simply hasn't caught up. Like Madonna, the 'Marilyn Munroe Without Tears' or that ultimate funky earth-mother Neneh Cherry, dancing hugely pregnant on 'Top of the Pops', singing her hit single 'Buffalo Stance' clad in tight black lycra, the New Woman had a confidence her older sisters could but envy; she didn't have to be self-consciously or stridently feminist because her feminism was *integrated* into her self-image. What a seductive picture – angst-free feminism! Even if premature, it embodied an overriding feminist dream that one day we would be able to wear our feminism unselfconsciously.

It is largely this confidence that accounts for *Elle*'s appeal rather than the belief held by many traditional feminists and large sections of the Left that women have simply been seduced by the dubious pleasures of consumption. Today the New Woman has an increasingly *sophisticated* response to fashion and the media. In an age where the notion of a coherent identity, 'the real self', is more and more unlikely and elusive, the idea that we can be manipulated in any straightforward way seems less and less credible. Fashion, far from being a source of oppression and manipulation of women, has become increasingly associated with strategies of resistance to fixed images of femininity.

Despite the orthodox left view that consumption cannot be radical in any circumstances, women have always had a complex relationship to consumption. Potentially both subversive and repressive, it has been represented as an opiate that kept the downtrodden Stepford wives in their fur-lined domestic prisons, but it has also been one of the few opportunities for the same women to express power and self-assertion.

In the early 1980s Feminism fell victim to its proscriptive legacy which dictated certain codes around dress, fashion and sexuality. Being a feminist had come to say more about what you didn't do – eat meat, fuck men, wear make-up – than what you did do. It is no surprise that 'eighties girl' is more attracted by the rhetoric of *laissez-faire* freedom that is so seductively presented by the Right.

She associates Feminism's proscriptive attitudes with the 'bossy' welfarism of the Labour years which was dismissed in the political climate of the 1980s as totally obsolete. So it is not feminism *per se* they reject but this morally authoritarian, feminist hegemony and the lifestyle associated with it.

For younger women part of the value and pleasure of consumption is the space it provides for transgressing traditional boundaries of sexual difference and for flouting anachronistic notions of femininity. It is true that older feminists saw themselves very much playing a counter-cultural role, resisting received ideas about feminity, but – as illustrated by the difference between the dungarees of the 1970s and the revival of the mini-skirt in the 1980s – younger women's approach to counter-cultural expression is more knowing and ironic, more attuned to popular culture. Consumption therefore became one of the essential ways in which younger women could assert their differences from another generation of feminists in the process of reclaiming the notions of pleasure and sensuality which had become taboo in the puritanism that gripped much of the feminist movement.

It is not therefore that younger women believe that to buy what you want is to be what you want (despite the urgings of the mass media), but that consumption has become associated with how we express our sense of freedom. In many ways, it has more eagerly responded to and reflected our discovery of the plurality of our identities and the value of cultural difference.

The Way we Were

It is ironic that Feminism should be having so much trouble with difference, because it was Feminism along with gay liberation, black activism and the other new social movements which pushed issues of difference into the spotlight in the first place. Through struggles for political recognition and personal validation, blacks, gays and women, succeeded in highlighting the problems of our notion of coherent individual 'identity', as well as the unitary, collective category of 'the people'. 'Man' – that tiny minority of white, middle-class, male bourgeoisie – was for the first time reflected at his rightful size, revealed in his minority status by that resounding

33

majority – those of us previously constructed as 'Other'. 'Nobody sees themselves as the centre anymore; everyone thinks they're on the margin' said Afro-American academic, Cornel West, summing up the impact of difference on all our lives.[2]

So how is it that despite paying lip-service to the importance of issues of difference (nowadays even the most established feminists journals are careful to speak in the plural about 'feminisms') that Feminism, unlike the practices of consumption, has been so ineffectual in taking ideas about difference on board or using them as the foundation of ideas for change?

Although Feminism, along with the other 'new movements' articulated around race, region and sexuality, rejected, resisted and ultimately undermined the identity of the traditional Left, they also emerged from that same eurocentric, liberal-humanist tradition of Western Enlightenment. In the process of its own 'becoming', Feminism came to reproduce the same universalist claims, the same *suppression* of difference, of that earlier, specifically socialist tradition.

Despite its great theoretical enthusiasm and its transformative potential, Feminism *along with* the traditional Left has failed to recognise or exploit the transformative potential of its own diverse constituency. As early as 1980 writers like Audre Lorde were pointing out how the ethnocentric, class- and age-specific perspective of the women's movement devalued its own authority and undermined feminism's intellectual vigour.

> to imply ... that all women suffer the same oppression because we are women, is to lose sight of the many and varied tools of patriarchy.[3]

As the 1980s unfolded the natural affinity between the traditional Left and its new movements became more and more strained – just as assumptions about women's 'global sisterhood' became less and less credible. Marginal women, those of a different race, class or generation struggled to see their own priorities represented on the feminist agenda but found much of Feminism as unresponsive to them as women had earlier found the mainstream Left (which had 'terrorised' women with their cries about 'true' socialism and 'real' agendas). As in the mainstream Left, particular priorities and (by extension) certain factions struggled to enshrine themselves as the one true Feminism. Many of us confronted with the emergent, feminist hierarchies were no longer sure whether it was about the liberation of all women or whether it was more pertinently about about the grasping and keeping of privilege by a tiny minority.

Just as the experiences of the new movements highlighted the inherent weaknesses of the sacred cows of Western Enlightenment, so marginal women's experience of oppression introduced themes which rendered invalid or incomplete the accepted feminist accounts of crucial issues like patriarchy, the family, work and reproduction.

Critical writings on ethnicity, had they been taken on board, offered a more sophisticated understanding of the complex articulation of race, class and gender. Though many contemporary Marxists acknowledged the importance of conceptualising race and gender as well as class structures and ideologies operating in society, this inherent weakness in theory meant that these issues were never felt as central. Instead they seemed simply 'tacked on', consigned to an ever shifting, nebulous and thoroughly opportunistic agenda that remained isolated from the heart of left practice and theory.

The practical costs of this failure, illustrated by the embittered battles within the Labour Party over, for example, Black Sections and a Women's Ministry, were a tendency to shunt certain issues into a hazy moral sphere rather than *incorporating* them into left discourse. Issues of racism and sexism – instead of being tackled on an institutional, societal basis – tended to be reduced to a personalised level, with individuals either deeply complacent or paralysed by guilt.

Like Marxism, psychoanalysis claimed to represent a universal, transcultural experience, but the insights of the new social movements have irrevocably relativised these claims. Ironically, Feminism – which played a crucial role in raising problems with these discourses – found itself replicating the same kind of absolutist ambitions in its own theoretical work. Feminist appropriations of psychoanalysis have contributed to many ideas about the acquisition of gender, but unfortunately these models do not account for culturally divergent experience between different groups of women, for example black and white (never mind those among, say, black women themselves). Female sexuality, for instance, as referred to in

35

most feminist literature is, by tacit assumption, white. Black women's sexuality if referred to at all, tends to be constructed as 'Other'.

These theoretical stumbling blocks were also associated with certain priorities that many women simply couldn't and wouldn't subscribe to. Non-white women, perhaps more conscious of the complex way in which forces of oppression interact, inevitably developed different perspectives. Conflicting attitudes to 'the family' provides an illustration of this problem. In the 1970s, socialist feminists appeared to have completely overlooked the power relations underlying racial oppression when formulating ideas about the family and the reproduction of labour power. Meanwhile radical feminists, demanding the death of the nuclear family, not only failed to perceive quite what a eurocentric model this demand was based on (white, patriarchal and nuclear), but also emerged with responses that simply could not be universally appropriate.

Neither socialist feminists nor radical feminists wanted to acknowledge that their concept of patriarchy failed to account for the power that white women in households historically had over some black men. Nor would they listen when the same women tried to point out that the family is not solely an oppressive institution: in fact, as black gay men have also recognised, in a white racist society, the family has often provided the only site of resistance and refuge.

The Personal is Political

The poverty of feminist theory had inevitable repercussions for the practical politics which seemed to be one of Feminism's great strengths. In their determination to reclaim their experiences, feminists, like their precursors in the black civil rights movement, placed great emphasis on personal experience and identity: the belief that you couldn't separate 'who you are from what you do' was at the centre of feminist struggles. This stress on 'authentic' experience and the attendant belief that 'the personal is political' represented a fundamental break from the traditional Left and proved extremely important in the way that it shifted the parameters of political life: politics became not just something you struggled with out there, in the world, but something to be dealt with in here, at home in one's private life. The radical potential of 'the personal is political' as a starting point which should unfailingly take us back into the world, is summed up by black activist June Jordan, in the introduction to her collection of essays *Civil Wars*:

> My life seems to be an increasing revelation of the intimate face of universal struggle. You begin with your family and the kids on the block, and next you open your eyes to what you call your people and that leads you into land reform into Black English into Angola leads you back to your own bed where you lie by yourself wondering if you deserve to be peaceful or trusted or desired or left to the freedom of your own unfaltering heart ... everything comes back to you.[4]

Instead, largely because many of the women who dominated Feminism were located in a very particular and privileged class and ethnic fraction, the exploration of the personal seemed to become *an end in itself*. But at what cost? Kobena Mercer asked this question in his contribution to the collection *Male Order: Unwrapping Masculinity*:

> The problem remains that while an honest examination of actual experience anchors the radical slogan 'the personal is political', what happens to the political if it goes no further than the purely personal?[5]

The answer can be found in the fate of many of the new movements, not just Feminism: Because of the class/ethnic composition of both the new social movements and much of the modern Left, this emphasis on inner feeling as the crucial component in shaping identity tended to be at the expense of, rather than in conjunction with, other external factors such as race. The radical potential of 'the personal is political', as a strategy which uniquely arms us to effect political change, simply didn't materialise. Encounter groups and consciousness raising seemed most pertinent to a privileged few, largely white and middle-class, who were lucky enough to be able to put to one side issues of race and class and who, by extension, had access through income and education to the somewhat esoteric discourses of psychotherapy and psychology. The result was a movement side-tracked by a peculiarly narcissistic dimension of 'the personal is political'.

Identity

Though therapy has proved valuable for some individuals from *all* sections of society, it has inevitably excluded and alienated many women, particularly black and working-class, who are disenfranchised from therapy as a lifestyle option and who find it hard to overcome their natural suspicion of the psychoanalytic discourses and treatments which have historically pathologised and abused them.

'The personal is political' was essential in providing connections between private experience and the public domain, but as an organisational form for sexual politics many of its practical manifestations were very limited, because they served a community privileged enough to find individual rather than collective solutions appropriate. Partly in response to this problem, the frustration of the subordinated voices, who were attempting to address the vicissitudes of the way power was held within the movement, led to the development of a kind of *inverted* hierarchy of privilege and value inside the feminist movement. As a counter-strategy to the white, middle-class women's movement which had tended to ignore or suppress issues of difference, the need to *insist* on difference became encoded, almost tabulated, in the politics of resistance and rhetoric of oppression of those who found themselves 'at the bottom of the pile', subordinated and marginalised.

The indirect consequence of the slogan 'the personal is political' was to create hierarchies of identities in which women, determined to prove their worthiness within the movement (and therefore to assert their right both to speak and be heard), competed against each other over the nature and extent of their oppressions. This exacerbated the separatist, centrifugal tendencies of the new movements in general, placing further stress on the relations between (for example) black and gay people, as well as among women themselves.

This simplistic, essentialist notion of political identity led to situations where appointing the odd, token woman/black/gay/lesbian to the appropriate committee or post was seen as sufficient by many organisations and individuals, not only to absolve themselves of accusations of racism/sexism/homophobia and so on, but also as a *general response* to these problems. This meant that a number of people became *professionally* black/gay/feminist and thus found themselves, usually unwittingly, 'appointed' as 'spokespeople' for their particular category of oppression.

The problem was not, in a strange way, that we took the implications of organising around identity too far, but that we didn't take it far enough. Had we really pushed this debate far enough we would have come to appreciate that we are all oppressor *and* oppressed. As June Jordan refreshingly declared when she 'counted herself out' of the feminist hierarchy:

> If I a black woman poet and writer, a professor of English, at State University, if I am oppressed then we need another word to describe a woman in a refugee camp in Palestine ... or any counterpart in South Africa.[6]

Instead of appreciating the interconnectedness of our oppressions we saw all our interests as mutually antagonistic, instead of making alliances we were in competition with one another. And since a large part of our energy was absorbed in a very particular brand of narcissism, it is no wonder that many (mainly younger) women were alienated from this often bickering, inward-looking and stagnant 'movement' – a house divided unto itself.

That was Then and This is Now

This feminist legacy can only be contrasted with the popular feminism which sells back to us a potent package of populist women's aspirations centred on having wider options, greater freedom and more autonomy, combined by many of the magazines with aggressively practical, campaigning approaches to issues like rape and child-care – and all this neatly wrapped up in a seductive cloak of designer difference. The New Woman of popular feminism may be a myth, but she is also in many ways an inspiration. There is nothing wrong with wanting to 'have it all'; it is only dangerous when we make the mistake of thinking we've got it. Without jettisoning her symbolic value we should remain aware of what is missing or excluded – that this dream applies only, if at all, within very narrow metropolitian confines, to women of a very specific class, race and age. Nor can popular feminism answer the real difficulties that will

Identity

beset this mythical creature when she shimmies down off the page: she can still suffer sexual harassment in the City or feel afraid parking her BMW. So even in fantasy, this woman cannot escape the consequences of women's subordination.

It is this disjuncture between what popular feminism can supply and what women really need that is the source of the curious mood of defeat which was so evident in *Cosmo's* January 1990 survey. On the one hand, we are told that we 'have it all' but on the other, we know that in many ways it is the same or harder than ever. Women are increasingly at risk of joining the growing underclass; if they are single parents, child-care provisions are still inadequate; we are still the 'carers' who have been left the responsibility to care for society's vulnerable and ill – the privatisation of care almost always means yet greater demands for unpaid work by women.

While women have no wish to return to the bosom of *the* feminist movement, with its dated lifestyle and connotations of puritanism, they do want these situations to change. But without some sort of campaigning 'movement' how do we go about changing them? For women consumption isn't the problem, though of course it isn't the answer either. There is a crisis of activism around the sort of issues which woman's magazines have capitalised on so successfully as a rallying point for a diverse readership (like today's debates about domestic violence). Women seem to have abandoned these discussions and struggles exclusively to the fate of women's page editorials.

Neither professional Feminism nor popular feminism, if isolated from each other, can hope to initiate the kind of collective activism that can effectively cope with the practical problems women are increasingly facing over, for example, maternity rights. If you believe as I do that optimism is not an option but a duty, then the time must be ripe for some sort of rapprochement. The opportunity will come from concrete issues, like the defence of women's right to choose which has so successfully mobilised huge numbers of American women against the Christian fundamentalists and others seeking to ban safe, legal abortion. Women have always found certain issues around which to mobilise and unite, which is not to say that all women share the same interests, just to remind us that *there are* interests we all share. Young or old, black or white, urban or rural, gay or straight, certain concerns belong to us all. We all want to be paid equal pay for equal work; we are all struggling for control of our sexual/reproductive rights; we are all concerned with the rising tide of violence against women; we all want appropriate maternity and domestic support.

Within and without the feminist movement it is time to map out some common territory. (It isn't only green politics that should remind us of our interdependency and vulnerability.) The limitations of organising around our oppressions have made us realise that women cannot effect lasting change in their lives without reference to men, any more than black people can change their situation independently of white people, gays in isolation from straights. Perhaps the 1990s is time to build bridges and create alliances, based not so much on fixed identities but on flexible *identifications*.

Of course this is easier said than done: 'consensus politics' so easily becomes 'lowest-common-denominator politics', with only the crudest and blandest of approaches ever gaining support. There is also the justifiable fear, particularly for certain marginal groups that the same old heirarchies will be reasserted and we will be submerged in each other's identities, rather than making alliances from a position of strength based on difference.

One of the features of our 'postmodern condition' which has most profoundly pushed back the advances of the 'new social movements' is that collective action has been replaced by individual salvation or, for some, damnation. Both strands of contemporary feminism – the professional and the popular – have fallen foul of, or failed to challenge, this privatisation of our social life. Frustration too has led to apathy, and by opting for the individualism of either 'subversive' shopping or personal career moves, feminism and Feminism have abandoned many goals and many areas of potential action. We seem to have forgotten that the activism of organising around issues was inspiring and empowering: we desperately need other models of political action than a vaguely progressive sort of consumerism (changing the world by buying a bottle of Ecover!), but without falling into the old trap of the divided movement syndrome – a politics unable to negotiate difference and so plagued by guilt and recrimination.

Identity

If the 1990s can be a decade which sees some kind of rapprochement between individual and collective responses to larger social problems, and if we can capitalise on the enormous, collective energy that popular feminism represents, then there will already have been a real improvement on the last ten years. It is an act of enlightened self-interest for us to heal the ruptures of the last few years. It is essential that a women's movement should, without assuming homogeneity or subsuming our own identities, genuinely get to grips with all its manifestations, from the popular to the professional, and begin to draw on all the range of women's divergent and complex experiences as it works towards a renewed agenda for change.

Notes

[1] Beatrix Campbell, *Cosmopolitan*, October 1989.
[2] From a lecture given as BFI visiting research fellow, entitled 'The New Black Politics of Cultural Difference', at the National Film Theatre, 23 June 1989.
[3] Audre Lorde, 'The Master's Tools Will Never Dismantle the Master's House', in *Moraga and Anzaldua*, 1981, p97.
[4] June Jordan, *Civil Wars*, Beacon Press, Boston 1981, xi.
[5] Kobena Mercer, in J. Rutherford and R. Chapman, *Male Order: Unwrapping Masculinity*, Lawrence & Wishart, London 1988, p121.
[6] Pratibha Parmar, 'Other Kinds of Dreams: an Interview with June Jordan', in *Spare Rib*, October 1987.

Welcome to the Jungle: Identity and Diversity in Postmodern Politics

KOBENA MERCER

Just now everybody wants to talk about 'identity'. As a keyword in contemporary politics it has taken on so many different connotations that sometimes it is obvious that people are not even talking about the same thing. One thing at least is clear – identity only becomes an issue when it is in crisis, when something assumed to be fixed, coherent and stable is displaced by the experience of doubt and uncertainty. From this angle, the eagerness to talk about identity is symptomatic of the postmodern predicament of contemporary politics.

The salient ambiguity of the word itself draws attention to the break-up of the traditional vocabulary of Left, Right and Centre. Our conventional maps are no longer adequate to the territory as the political landscape has been radically restructured over the last decade by the hegemony of the New Right. Hence, in no uncertain terms, the 'identity crisis' of the Left. After ten years of Thatcherism, the attitudes, assumptions and institutions of the British Left have been systematically demoralised, disorganised and disaggregated. Neo-liberal hegemony has helped to transform the political terrain to the point where the figurative meaning of the Left/Right dichotomy has been totally reversed. This was always a metaphor for the opposition between progressive and reactionary forces, derived in fact from the seating arrangements of the General Assemblies after the French Revolution. But today the word 'revolution' sounds vaguely embarrassing when it comes out of the mouths of people on

43

the Left: it only sounds as if it means what it says when uttered in the mouths of the radicalised Right. In the modern period, the Left anticipated the future with an optimistic attitude, confident that socialism would irreversibly change the world. Today such epic beliefs seem to be disappearing into the grand museum, as it is the postmodern Right that wants to 'revolutionise' the entire society and remake our future in its own millenial image of neo-liberal market freedom.

The identity crisis of the Left is underlined not only by the defeat experienced by trade unions and other organisations that make up the labour movement, but above all by the inability of the Labour Party to articulate an effective 'opposition'. Even so, the problem goes beyond the official theatre of parliamentary democracy. The classical Marxist view of the industrial working classes as the privileged agent of revolutionary historical change has been undermined and discredited from below by the emergence of numerous social movements – feminisms, black struggles, national liberation, anti-nuclear and ecological movements – that have also reshaped and redefined the sphere of politics. The ambiguity of 'identity' serves in this regard as a way of acknowledging the presence of new social actors and new political subjects – women, black people, lesbian and gay communities, youth – whose aspirations do not neatly fit into the traditional Left/Right dichotomy. However I am not so sure that 'identity' is what these movements hold in common: on the contrary, within and between the various 'new' movements that have arisen in postwar Western capitalist democracies what is asserted is an emphasis on 'difference'. In a sense the 'newness' of these struggles consists precisely in the fact that such differences cannot be coded or programmed into same old formula of Left, Right and Centre. The proliferation of differences is highly ambivalent as it relativises the Big Picture and weakens the totalising universal truth claims of ideologies like Marxism, thus demanding acknowledgement of the *plural* sources of oppression, unhappiness and antagonism in contemporary capitalist societies.

On the other hand, the downside of such diversification and fragmentation is the awareness that there is no necessary relationship between these new social movements and the traditional labour movement, or to put it another way, it cannot be taken for granted that there is common cause in the project of creating a socialist society. This question arises with a double sense of urgency, not only because it has become difficult to imagine what a socialist society looks like as something 'totally' different from any other type of society, but because the new social subjects have no necessary belonging on either side of the distinction between progressive and reactionary politics, which is to say they could go either way.

GLC: Difference and Division

I want to examine the unwieldy relationship between the Left and the new social movements because they both share problems made symptomatic in terms of 'identity' and yet there is no vocabulary in which to conduct a mutual dialogue on the possibility of alliances or coalitions around a common project, which is the starting point for any potentially hegemonic strategy. This dilemma was forcefully brought to light in the experiments in municipal socialism led by the Greater London Council and other metropolitan local authorities in Britain in the early to mid-1980s. Such initiatives mobilised popular enthusiasm for socialist politics, but now that the whole experience is a fast-fading memory what is mostly remembered is the mess created by the micro-antagonisms that erupted precisely in the relationship between the traditional Left and the political movements articulated around race, gender, ethnicity and sexuality.

The scenario of fragmentation that emerged was further dramatised by the conflictual differences within and between the new social movements themselves. The tabloid discourse of 'Loony Leftism' picked up on this state of affairs and created a reactive populist parody to which the Labour leadership readily capitulated. In the aftermath of a local campaign for 'Positive Images' of lesbians and gays in Haringey schools in 1987, the Labour Party dissociated itself from the GLC's somewhat ragged rainbow coalition with the dismissive and divisive remark, 'the lesbian and gay issue is costing us dear among the pensioners'. The 'London factor' was held to be responsible for yet another electoral defeat, but in the search for something to blame Labour not only rationalised its unwillingness to

45

construct new alliances, but helped pave the way for the hateful, authoritarian logic of Clause 28. Why couldn't Labour articulate pensioners *and* lesbians and gays within the same discourse? Was it not conceivable that pensioners and lesbians and gay men might even have a common interest in constructing an alternative to the unremitting 'new reality' of Thatcherite Britain?

What was important and exciting about the GLC in that briefly optimistic moment around 1983 was precisely the attempt to find forms of democratic representation and participation that would be responsive to the diversity of social identities active in the contemporary polity. Looking back, was it any wonder the experiment failed given that *this was the first time it had ever been contemplated*? The question of alliances between the labour movement, the Left and the various new social movements arose in the 1970s in trade union strikes, single-issue protest campaigns, localised community action and cultural mobilisations such as Rock Against Racism. While these experiences helped to create a fragile network of association either in the workplace or in civil society, the GLC experiment attempted to re-mobilise alliances around a socialist programme *within* the institutional spaces of the local state. The shift was important because of the symbolic and material resources invested in local government as an apparatus of the state, but by the same token it proved impossible to translate the connections between the various elements once they were 'inside' the bureaucratic machinery of 'representative democracy'.

The Labour Left administration of the 1981-86 GLC was the first of its kind to take the demands of the new movements seriously and to go beyond the tokenistic management of noisy 'minorities'. Conversely, this was the first time many community-based activists operated within the framework of officialdom, whereas their previous extra-parliamentary 'autonomy' made them sceptical of having anything to do with it. What happened when the two came face to face was that expectations about equal participation and representation in decision-making were converted into sectional demands and competing claims about the legitimation of different needs. The possibility of coalitions was pre-empted by the competitive dynamic of who would have priority access to resources.

The worst aspects of the new social movements emerged in a

rhetoric of 'identity politics' based on an essentialist notion of a fixed hierarchy of racial, sexual or gendered oppressions. By playing off each other to establish who was more authentically oppressed than whom, the residual separatist tendencies of the autonomous movements played into the normative calculation of 'disadvantage' inscribed in welfare statism. For their part, the generation of new Left activists who became the managers of state bureaucracy could only take over rather than transform the traditional top-down conception of meeting needs. Hence official rhetoric acknowledged diversity in a discourse of 'race, class and gender' which became the policy repertoire in which each element was juggled about and administered according to expediency, patronage and good old Labourite pragmatism. The rationing of meagre resources became a means of regulating and controlling 'difference' because, as the various actors perceived it, one group's loss was another group's gain. In this zero-sum game the only tangible consequence of diversity was dividedness.

I've chosen to situate the two faces of 'identity' (both as the Left's general crisis of agency and as the shortcomings of the GLC) because what calls for thinking is the belatedness of the convergence. Why did it take so long for the Left and the new social movements to come together around the basic questions of civic democracy? If nothing else, the 'failure' of the GLC to construct common ground highlights a legacy of combined and uneven development in the postwar period. My impression is that since the 1960s there has been a cosy but vague assumption that there is a 'natural affinity' between the autonomous 'liberation' movements and the ultimate goals of the labour movement in that a shared conception of democratic equality and freedom sets them both against mainstream conservatism and the hierarchical inequalities of the capitalist status quo. The lesson of the GLC is that this is not necessarily so. What is at stake is not only a legacy of mistrust, suspicion and even hostility between the parties, organisations and unions that make up 'the Left' and the more dispersed and diffused elements of black community struggles, the women's movement, gay and lesbian movements and the ecology movement, but the fact that if radical democratic alliances are not constructed by and for the Left, such alliances will turn up in favour of the Right.

Identity

The absence of a common language in which to conceive contemporary alliances among potentially counter-hegemonic forces is a fundamental problem that needs to be acknowledged. Difference and diversity are values which are not particularly well practised on the traditional Left. Confronted by the real implications of political diversity, the Marxist tradition reveals its impoverished condition as the monologic concept of class struggle is inadequate to the plurality of conflicts and antagonisms at work in contemporary society. Classical Marxism is simply deaf to the dialogic noise produced by the diverse voices, interests and identities that make up contemporary politics. On the other hand, the weaknesses of the new movements are equally demoralising: without a broader view of social transformation the movements around race, gender and sexuality are not only vulnerable to co-option and appropriation within the existing capitalist order, but can be articulated with the reactionary project of the New Right itself. Under the conditions of capitalist modernisation and social-democratic consensus in the 1950s, 60s and 70s, it might have been plausible to make the assumption that there was indeed the possibility of a broadly 'Left' alliance between the labour movement and the new social movements. Today, however, we need to contend with and be capable of understanding the deeply reactionary character of the 'broad democratic alliances' that have turned up not only among the old social actors, but between the new social actors – women, black people, gays – and the neo-conservative Right. Consider the tendencies at work in the contradictions of the Haringey scenario.

The campaign was based on a perceived equivalence in the discourse of 'Positive Images'. This concept emerged in multicultural education in the 1970s as a result of black struggles against under-achievement which were then neutralised and accommodated within a liberal pluralist conception of cultural diversity. In taking up the slogan against homophobic practices, lesbian and gay activists conducted legitimate arguments for educational equality but in a form that was compromised by its opportunistic appropriation from the politics of race and ethnicity. The problem was in turn compounded by the reaction against the initiative, articulated by the Parents' Rights Group and other local pressure groups, including the Haringey Black Pressure Group on Education whose spokesman argued that 'homosexuality is something that has been introduced into our culture by Europeans: it is an unnatural set of acts that tend toward genocide'.[1] Influenced by this rhetoric of denial, black parents participated alongside the New Patriotic Movement whose banner slogan, 'Gays = Aids = Death', set up a more powerful system of equivalences. Homophobia became hegemonic over racism as the more important source of support for the mobilisation of right-wing populism, framed on a wider scale in the public sphere by the 'enemies within' logic of tabloid 'Loony Leftism'. Was it a paradox of the postmodern condition or just everyday life in post-colonial Britain that what resulted was an 'unthinkable' alliance between black people and the National Front? Welcome to the jungle, welcome to the politics of indeterminacy in the twilight of modernity.

Like 'identity', difference, diversity and fragmentation are keywords in the postmodern vocabulary where they are saturated with groovy connotations. But it should be clear that there is nothing particularly groovy about the postmodern condition at all. As a bestseller ideology in artistic and intellectual circles the postmodern paradigm has been and gone, but as a pervasive sensibililty in everyday life its smelly ideological effect lingers on. Postmodernism means many different things to many different people, but the key motifs of displacement, decentring and disenchantment have a specific resonance and relevance for the Left and new social movements after the demoralising decade of Thatcherism.

In philosophical terms, postmodernism has been discussed as a weakening, fading or relativisation of the absolutist or universalist values of the Western Enlightenment. The master narratives are collapsing, which is to say we no longer have the confidence to invest belief in the foundational myths of inevitable human rationality or social progress. Certain intellectuals however (like Baudrillard) are apt to exaggerate the effect in a rather stupefied apocalyptic manner simply because they can no longer adopt the universalist postures they once did. Just like the organised Left, a whole generation of postwar intellectuals have been thrown into identity crisis as philosophies of Marxism and Modernism have begun to lose their adversarial aura. The loss of faith in the idea of a cultural avant-garde parallels the crisis of credulity in now discredited notions of political vanguardism or 'scientific socialism'. But the narcissistic pathos expressed within the prevailing postmodern ideology obscures the more generalised effect of decentring acknowledged in common sense. Everybody intuitively knows that everyday life is so complex that no singular belief-system or Big Story can hope to explain it all. We don't need another hero. But we do need to make sense of the experiences that characterise postmodern structures of feeling.

In sociological terms, this means a recognition of the fragmentation of traditional sources of authority and identity, the displacement of collective sources of membership and belonging such as 'class' and 'community' that help to construct political loyalties, affinities and identifications. One doesn't need to invoke the outmoded base/superstructure metaphor to acknowledge the impact of deterritorialised and decentralised forms of production in late modern capitalism. While certain structures associated with the highly centralised logic of mass production and mass consumption give way to more flexible transnational arrangements that undermine the boundaries of the sovereign nation-state, other boundaries become more rigid, such as those that exclude the late modern underclass from participation in free-market choices – 'you can have anything you want, but you better not take it from me'.[2] The New Right is not the origin of these changes, but the brutalising neo-conservative reassertion of competitive individualism and archaic 'Little Englandism' has hegemonised the common-sense terms in which the British are invited to make sense of and live through the vertiginous experience of displacement and decentring that these processes entail. It is here that we arrive at the political terms of postmodernism in the sense that Thatcherism represents a new type of hegemony which has totally displaced the mythical 'Centre' of the postwar social-democratic consensus.

Identity is a key motif of post-consensus politics because the postwar vocabulary of Left, Right and Centre, in which individual and collective subjects identified their loyalties and commitments, has been shot to pieces. The decentring of the social-democratic consensus, which was historically constructed around the axioms of welfare-state capitalism, was partly the result of its own internal economic and political contradictions. But as Stuart Hall's analysis of

Thatcherism has shown, it was the neo-liberal agenda of 'free market and strong state', crystallised in the mid-1970s, that took the lead in answering the task of reconstructing a new form of popular consent by creating a new form of governmentality.[3] If one identifies 1968 as the turning point in the deepening crisis of social-democratic consensus, it can be said that it was the New Right, not the New Left nor the new social movements, that won out historically. It is precisely for this reason that we need to undertake an archeology of the recent past in which the problematic relationship between the Left and the new social movements developed.

Children of the Revolution

> And my brother's back at home, with his Beatles and his Stones, We never got it off on that revolution stuff, What a drag, Too many snags.
> 'All the Young Dudes'[4]

One way of clarifying what is at stake in the postmodern is to point out that the grammatical prefix 'post' simply means the noun it predicates is 'past'. The ubiquitous prefix thus suggests a generalised mood or sensibility which problematises the past in relation to the contemporary horizon from which we imagine the future. Jacques Donzelot has characterised this as a new 'apprehension of time' [5] resulting from the exhaustion of the rational myth of progress: new future or no future, adapt or die, that's how it feels, especially on the Left and among all the oppositional movements that once thought that time was on our side. In this sense, as a shift in popular memory that results in a changed disposition towards the past, one recognises that the cultural forms of postmodernism – the pervasive mode of a retro/nostalgia/recycling aesthetic, the prevalence of pastiche and parody – are implicated in a logic that problematises the recent past by creating ironic distance between 'then' and 'now'. The sixties and seventies are effectively historicised in much the same way as historians treat 'the twenties' or 'the forties'. What happened the day before yesterday now looks like it happened a long time ago, and sometimes it looks as if it never happened at all. While ex-leftist intellectuals are eager to repudiate and renounce the radical fantasies of '1968', a more generalised process of erasure and effacement is at work, selectively wiping out certain traces of the recent past sedimented in common sense by the progressive gains of the sixties.

Taking this analysis a step further, Lawrence Grossberg has suggested a reading of the postmodern sensibility as a crucial resource in New Right hegemony. Neo-conservatism dominates our ability to imagine the future by performing on the postmodern 'frontier-effect' in popular memory. Although it is addressed to the experience of Reaganism in the USA, it pertains to the British experience as Grossberg argues that the sense of disillusionment with the radical aspirations of the 1960s is central to the mobilisation of popular support for the neo-liberal programme of structuring the state and civil society in the present:[6]

> If the state hegemonic project of the New Right entails deconstructing the postwar social democratic consensus, its cultural hegemonic project entails disarticulating the central relationship between the national identity, a specific set of generational histories, and the equation of the national popular with postwar youth culture.

One only has to recall those images of Harold Wilson and The Beatles (fresh from Buckingham Palace with their OBE's) to appreciate the resonance of the equation between postwar modernisation in Western capitalist democracies and the cultural presence of a new social subject, the teenager. In this equation 'youth' came to embody the promise of modernity within the ethos of social democracy. Grossberg argues that the repudiation of capitalist modernisation within the youth counter-culture of the late 1960s marked the cut-off point or a threshold of dissensus against the Centre. The neo-conservative onslaught against 'the sixties' has since become a crucial component in winning consent for neo-liberal democracy, or as Francis Pym once said, 'I think public expectations are too high. We have an end to the language of the Sixties. Today we have got to rid ourselves of these outlooks and look at economic and social matters in a new light'.[7]

During its period of opposition in the 1970s Thatcherism mobilised a frontier-effect which polarised the political field into two antagonistic positions. Labourism was identified with the interventionist state, while the Tories positioned themselves 'out there' with the people, against the state, to recruit support for a market-led definition of freedom detached from the welfarist conception of equality.[8] Since 1979 the Tories have never stopped using the state to pursue monetarist economic policies, but as an ideology that has now achieved considerable hegemony in official institutions and popular common sense Thatcherism seeks to maintain its sources of support by playing on a binary polarity in which the Left is identified with the past and the Right monopolises the imaginary horizon of the future. There can be no return to the bad old days of dissensus, which is to say that in popular consciousness the possibility of a future for socialism is rendered 'unthinkable' because the popular image of the Left is fixed in 'the winter of discontent', a vestige of the past which occasionally flickers up in television documentaries.

The 'active forgetting' of the recent past is further underlined by Thatcherite identity politics in which 'Little Englandism', the peculiarly English combination of racism, nationalism and populism, becomes the predominant framework of the imagined community in which the 'collective will' is constructed – 'its great to be Great again', as the 1987 Tory election slogan put it. The Falklands War and Royal Weddings, Victorian values and Raj nostalgia movies are all recycled in the Great British heritage industry, and not just for the benefit of Japanese or American tourists either. Workers in Sunderland or Derbyshire know that their futures might well depend on decisions taken in Tokyo or Chicago, but the British don't like to think of themselves as a Third World nation run on a service economy. So the nation is enjoined to travel back to the future in a rewriting of history which leapfrogs over the recent past in order to retrieve an entirely fictional image of systemic 'national-popular' unity based on the revival and recycling of the wretched age of Empire.

Dick Hebdige has called this 'digging for Britain'[9] in that historicity and popular conceptions of the past have become a key site in which the changed circumstances of the present are apprehended and defined. One only has to consider the retrieval of historical counter-memory in black pop culture (where the cut 'n' mix aesthetic informs the narration of stories precisely hidden from history in the dominant discourse of the past) to recognise the sources of popular resistance to the postmodern frontier-effect, something underlined in a recent comment by the pop group 'Tears for Fears':[10]

> The Tories are renowned for evoking memories of the Victorian era cos it falls in line with their paternalistic morality. What I wanted to do was bring back memories of that era when Britain was 'great' – the era of Harold Wilson, The Beatles, the red London bus, Twiggy and the mini … There was a time when it was okay to be idealistic or, dare I say it, spiritual. And I wanted to jog everybody's memory.

A few years ago Judith Williamson rightly criticised a simple-minded left-wing populism which merely imitated and capitulated to neo-conservative definitions of popularity, and indeed one might also note a tendency towards culturalism or 'cultural substitutionism' among Left intelligensia for whom 'postmodernism' means just going to the shops.[11] In one sense this is symptomatic of the Left's deeply demoralising experience of being actively disarticulated as a result of the postmodern frontier-effect. The withdrawal and retreat into culturalism further underlines another ironic reversal of the Thatcher decade as cultural studies has been appropriated into a knowledge-producing apparatus that services the reproduction of hyper-consumption in the culture industry.

These indicative signs of the times underscore the identity crisis of the Left, but the *contradictoriness* of the postmodern requires a *relational* emphasis because what is experienced as a loss of identity and authority in some quarters is also an empowering experience which affirms the identities and experiences of others *for precisely the same reasons*. The 1980s have seen a significant renewal and revitalisation of black politics. Whether this has occurred despite Thatcherism or because of it, issues of race and ethnicity have been irrevocably inscribed on the national political agenda, a process which represents a considerable advance on the previous decades. Indeed, if I think about the intensity of all those discussions about 'the definition of black' which occurred in the post-1981 scenario after the 'inner-city' riots, the experience of decentring has been highly empowering as it has also articulated an experience of de-marginalisation in which new forms of collective subjectivity and 'imagined community' have been mobilised by various political and cultural activities.

Welcome to the Jungle

What was so important about the demand for 'black representation' that could be heard in Britain in the early 1980s was an extension of radical democracy in which a marginalised and subordinate group affirmed and asserted their rights to representation within political society. The shift from 'ethnic minority' to 'black' registered in the language of political discourse demonstrated a process in which the objects of racist ideology reconstituted themselves as subjects of social, cultural and political change, actively making history albeit under circumstances not of their own choosing. A minority is literally a minor, not simply the abject and dependent child-like figure necessary for the legitimation of paternalistic ideologies of assimilation and integration, but a social identity that is *in-fans*, without a voice, debarred and disenfranchised from access to political representation in a liberal or social democracy. The rearticulation of black as a political rather than racial category among Asian, Caribbean and African people, originating from a variety of ethnic backgrounds and sharing common experiences of British racism, thus created a new form of symbolic 'unity' out of the signifiers of racial difference. For over four centuries the sign /black/ had nothing but negative connotations as it signified racialised identity within Manichean dualism, an absolute division between 'the West' and 'the Rest' in which the identity of the black subject was negated as Other, ugly and ultimately un-human. The decentring of 'Man', the centred subject of Western liberal humanism, is nothing if not a good thing as it has radically demonstrated the coercive force and power implicated in the wordly construction of the Western rational *cogito* – the subject of logocentrism and all the other 'centrisms' that construct its representations of reality. 'Man' consisted of a subject whose identity and subjectivity depend on the negation, exclusion and denial of Others. Women, children, slaves, criminals, madmen and savages were all alike in as much as their otherness affirmed 'his' identity as the universal norm represented in the category 'human'. Indeed, if the period after the modern is when the others of modernity talk back, what is revealed is the fictional character of Western universality, as the subject who arrogated the power to speak on behalf of humanity was nothing but a minority himself – the hegemonic white male bourgeois subject whose centred identity depended on the othering of subordinate class, racial, gendered and sexual subjects who were thereby excluded from the category 'human' and marginalised from the democratic right to a political subjectivity.

I've chosen to situate the rearticulation of black identity in this way because this specific historical experience exemplifies what we need from 'theory'. Back in the late 1970s as an undergraduate at art school I felt terrorised by the authoritative postures of the intellectual avant-garde associated with Althusserian 'scientificity'. At the height of 'high theory' I felt that the esoteric, elitist language of *Screen* did nothing to empower me, although I recognised that something important and relevant to my needs was being articulated in the passionate debates over ideology, representation and subjectivity. At the time, confronted by texts like *Language and Materialism*, I was simply bewildered by the thesis that 'the subject is constituted in language',[12] but now that the dogma and rigidity of intellectual attitudinising have thankfully waned and faded I feel it is paradoxically necessary actually to conserve and defend the 'commitment to theory', not least of all against the cynical indifference and 'anything goes' pluralism of postmodern ideology. In this respect the radicalisation of black politics in the 1980s dramatises the post-structuralist thesis that subjectivity is indeed reconstituted in language as it is precisely the antagonistic articulation of the same signifier /black/ that highlights politics as a practice of articulation of elements which in themselves have no intrinsic progressive or reactionary character; it all depends on the signifying chain of the political discourse in which they are articulated and represented. As Stuart Hall has argued:

> Sometimes, the class struggle in language occurred between two different terms: the struggle, for example, to replace the term 'immigrant' with the term 'black'. But often, the struggle took the form of a different accenting of the same term: eg. the process by means of which the derogatory colour 'black' became the enhanced value 'black' (as in 'Black is Beautiful') ... In the discourse of the Black movement, the denigratory connotation 'black = the despised race' could be inverted into its opposite: 'black = beautiful' ... [this was] every bit as 'real' or 'material' as so-called non-ideological practices because it effected their outcome. It was 'real' because it was real in its effects. It was determinate, because it depended on other conditions being fulfilled. 'Black' could not be converted to 'black is beautiful' simply by wishing it

56

so. It had to become part of an organised practice of struggles requiring the building up of black resistances as well as the development of new forms of black consciousness.[13]

Volosinov's pre-structuralist philosophy of language emphasised the multi-accentual character of the keywords at stake in hegemonic struggle as competing voices and positions struggle to articulate and accentuate poly-vocal signs into one direction rather than another.[14] Like Hall, Ernesto Laclau and Chantal Mouffe have adapted the insights of this relational approach to Gramsci's strategic conception of hegemonic struggle as a 'war of position' in which contending forces seek to win the consent of the 'collective will' in the process of constructing forms of subjectivity and consciousness in common sense. Social identities are structured 'like a language' in that they can be articulated into a range of contradictory positions from one discursive context to the next since each element in ideology and consciousness has no necessary belonging in any one political code or system of representation. As Hall argues, 'What was being struggled over was not the 'class belongingness' of the term [black], but the inflexion it could be given, its connotative field of reference'.[15]

Laclau's analytic framework is organised at a rather frustrating level of theoretical abstraction, but by recognising the partial and incomplete character of politicised identities such 'discourse-theory' eschews universalist claims in favour of mapping out the historically specific conjunctures in which hegemonic strategy constructs 'imaginary unities' out of the diverse and heterogeneous positions which individual and collective subjects actually occupy in their lived experience. The postmodern riddle of political subjectivity – what do a trade unionist, a Tory, a racist, a Christian, a wife-beater and a consumer have in common? – *they can all be the same person*,[16] provides cold comfort for those who assume that 'the politics of identity' is simply fun and games. It also undermines the unhelpful dichotomy between old social movements, such as the labour movement, and the new social movements because it insists that 'the working classes' are not constituted purely by economic practices alone but through complex power relations that derive from relations of gender, generation, region, nationality and race as much as class relations derived from the mode of production. This relational view enjoys some degree of circulation today, but we also need to go beyond the mere concatenation of particularism implicit in the all-too-familiar mantra of 'race, gender, ethnicity, sexuality' (even though the economistic perspective of traditional Labourism makes such acknowledgement necessary) if we are to grasp the conflicts and contradictions that exist within and between each of these various identities in play in contemporary politics.

1968: What did you do in the war, Daddy?

Chantal Mouffe has brought such tasks into focus by calling for the 'institutionalisation of a true pluralism' which recognises and respects the diversified character of political struggles which have radicalised democracy in postwar capitalist societies. By grounding her analysis of 'new democratic struggles' in terms of a view which emphasises the processes that enable or prevent the extension of the subversive logic of democratic 'equality', she argues that

> The progressive character of a struggle does not depend on its place of origin ... but rather on its link with other struggles. The longer the chain of equivalences set up between the defence of the rights of one group and those of other groups, the deeper will be the democratisation process and the more difficult it will be to neutralise certain struggles or make them serve the ends of the Right. The concept of solidarity can be used to form such a chain of democratic equivalences.[17]

Laclau's metaphorical concept of 'frontier-effects' refers precisely to the formation of imaginary unities and political solidarities, crystallised out of numerous micro-alliances or systems of equivalence, that polarise the political field into democratic antagonism. The 'them and us' logic of authoritarian populism and the paranoid policing of the 'enemy within' articulated by Thatcherite ideology represents one such frontier-effect that has hegemonised popular consciousness in the present. But to understand the effectiveness of this right-wing closure (which largely explains why the Left is so defeated and demoralised) we have to grasp the reversals by which the New Right disarticulated and rearticulated the emancipatory identifications which the democratic revolution inaugurated by new social movements opened up against the 'Centre' in the postwar period.

As Mouffe notes, forms of oppression and inequality based on racism and patriarchy pre-date industrial capitalism, but the contradictory development of democracy within the universalised 'commodification' of social relations in the postwar period was one of the key conditions by which the demand for equality was radicalised in the politics of race and gender. Just like women, the colonised participated equally in the war effort against Fascism and in this respect were interpellated as 'equal' by one set of discourses, while the terms of postwar consensus repositioned them – in the labour process, in the political process, in social relations – once more as 'unequal'. Mouffe argues that this contradictory interpellation created the conditions for new forms of democratic antagonism not because people 'naturally' aspire towards freedom, equality and solidarity but because such values were placed at the centre of social and political life by social democracy which nevertheless denied such values to its subordinated subjects and marginalised citizens. It is from this perspective that 'we can see the widening of social conflict as the extension of the democratic revolution into more and more spheres of social life'.[18] It seems to me that a historical reading of this concrete conjuncture would reveal the *privileged* metaphor of 'race' within the radicalisation of the postmodern democratic imaginary.

At one level this is acknowledged globally in the geopolitical metaphor of First, Second and Third Worlds. In the context of the Cold War, whose 'Iron Curtain' polarised two rival superpowers, the assertion of US hegemony in a new phase of multinational capitalism required the presence of the underdeveloped world to stabilise and reproduce the logic of modernisation necessary to the existence of the overdeveloped world. But politically speaking the Third World was brought into existence by the anti-colonial struggles of the colonised, by the historical presence of subjects who were formerly objects of imperialism. In such movements as Pan-Africanism or Ghandi's non-violent mobilisation on the Indian subcontinent, localised regional, ethnic and 'tribal' identities were hegemonised by revolutionary nationalism. Western forms of nationhood were appropriated and articulated with 'syncretic' traditionalism and indigenous 'folklore' to encode the demand of new collective historical subjects for democratic independence, self-determination and liberation. In Kwame Nkrumah's speculations about the existence of an 'African personality' and in Frantz Fanon's diagnosis of the political unconscious of racism (and the psychic reality of its 'superiority/inferiority complex' as constitutive of black/white subjectivities[19]) what we see is not the description of pre-existing, already formed identities but an intellectual reflection on the transformative practices, made possible by new democratic antagonisms, that were bringing new forms of collective subjectivity into being. Aside from the chain of equivalence constructed within the colonial nation-states seeking liberation, we also see an extension of the same process within the metropolitan First World in terms of the radicalised demand for autonomy.

The Afro-American civil rights movement in the United States during the 1950s and early 1960s acted as the catalyst in which the radical democratic chain of equivalence reconstituted political subjects across the metaphorical boundary of racial difference itself. On the one hand, this unfolded internally as a radicalisation of subaltern racial identity inscribed in the transition from 'Negro' to 'Black'. The reformist character of Martin Luther King's leadership, through which the demand for equal citizenship rights was articulated, was transformed in the urban setting by nationalist ideologies, such as those advocated by Malcolm X, to extend beyond legal and social rights into an existential affirmation of a negated subjectivity (exactly that which was designated under erasure as simply 'X'). This resulted in the mid-1960s in the highly indeterminate and volatile metaphor of 'black power'. As Manning Marable has pointed out, this rallying cry was articulated into right-wing positions (even President Nixon became an advocate as he endorsed it as a form of black capitalism) as well as the left-wing positions associated with the Black Panther Party and its charismatic leadership which , for a brief moment around the late 1960s, became a counter-hegemonic subject capable of leading and directing a range of positions into the chain of radical democratic equivalence.[20]

One of the factors behind this process lay in the trans-racial identifications by which the codified symbols and imaginary metaphors of 'black liberation' were taken up, translated and rearticulated among postwar generations of white youth. Among student activists, within the bohemian 'underground', within second-wave feminism and in the nascent gay liberation movement, the signs and signifiers of radical blackness were appropriated into a chain of equivalences that empowered subordinate identities within *white* society. Of course, this most often took a cultural rather than conventionally political form of solidarity. The mass diffusion of black expressive culture through the pop and rock music industry played a critical role in the dissemination of such imaginary modes of alternative identification, culminating in the 1969 Woodstock Festival where the predominantly white, middle-class youth that gathered thought they constituted a nation within the nation, a new imagined community. In psychedelic Britain this was the imaginary space in which representations of an 'alternative society' were constructed. Here we see the vicissitudes of ambivalence, inversion and othering in the political identifications made possible by the cultural forms of antagonism which articulated the extension of the radical democratic system of equivalences. At its liminal point whiteness was emptied out in a direct imitation of empowered black subjectivity, such as when the activist John Sinclair formed the short-lived White Panther Party in the United States in 1968.[21]

Some of the contradictions inherent in the unfolding of this system of equivalences became apparent both at the frontier with the 'law and order' state (which effectively wiped out and repressed the guerilla strategies of the far Left) and within the counter-culture itself, where the masculinist character of such anti-authoritarianism was contested by women and gay men. But in this respect, the radicalisation of sexual politics from 1970 onwards derived significant momentum from imaginary equivalences with black struggle, as 'black pride' and 'brotherhood' acted as metonymic leverage for the affirmation of 'gay pride' and the assertion that 'sisterhood is strength'. Finally, although it should be pointed out that such radicalisation also affected the increasing militancy of the labour movement in the early 1970s, in the context of the poly-vocal anti-consensus populism of the period it was the New Right, and not the New Left nor the new social movements, that got hold of what the Situationists used to call the 'reversible connecting factor'.

The privileged metaphor of 'race' was also crucial to the

emergence of a neo-conservative populism which, in Britain, was articulated in 1968 by the dramatic interventions of Enoch Powell. Volosinov noted that 'the social multi-accentuality of the sign ... has two faces, like Janus', and that 'this inner dialectic quality of the sign comes out fully into the open only in times of social crises or revolutionary changes' because 'in ordinary circumstances ... the ideological sign in an established dominant ideology ... always tries to stabilise the dialectical flux'.[22] In his speeches on race and nation, culminating in the 'Enemies Within' in 1970, Powell encoded the dialectical flux of the crisis of authority into a populist chain of equivalences in which issues of race and immigration opened up a broader ideological attack against the Centre, destabilising the values of social democracy. As an advocate of free-market capitalism and a staunch defender of the primacy of the nation-state in politics, Powell prefigured and helped pave the way for the logic of authoritarian populism we now know as Thatcherism.[23] But what also needs acknowledging is the fact that the three lines of force which divided the field of political antagonism between the new social movements, the New Left and the New Right were implicated in the *same* struggle over the 'communifying' logic of democratic equivalences, set in motion by the decentring of consensus. What is at issue in the moment of 1968 is an understanding of how these three nuclei of political identification competed for the collective will of society. Contrary to the impression given by academic deconstructionists, the moment of indeterminacy, undecidability and ambivalence is never a neutral or purely textual affair – it is when politics is experienced at its most intense.

As someone who was eight years old in 1968 I have no direct experience, memory or investment on which to draw, as more recent dates like 1976 or 1981 punctuate more formative experiences in the historical construction of my own subjectivity. Yet precisely as a cultural text in popular memory, '1968' has an affective resonance that I feel needs to be defended and conserved against the 'active forgetting' which the contemporary postmodern frontier-effect encourages. What is demanded by the shift in popular memory is not a history that aims to 'articulate the past the way it really was', but a mode of story-telling which, in Walter Benjamin's phrase, aims to 'seize hold of a memory as it flashes up at a moment of danger'.[24] In lieu of a concrete historical account of the postmodern crisis of social democracy (which should be backdated to the period between 1956 and 1968), my sketch of radical democratic subjectivities is really only an inventory arising out of my own experiences growing up in the imaginary of the post-'68 conjuncture. Nevertheless, by asking 'whatever happened to the empowering identifications of the sixties?' we might arrive at a clearer idea of why the 1980s have been so awful.

Between the Fragments: Citizenship in a Decentred Society

> We no longer regard ourselves as the successive incarnations of the absolute spirit – Science, Class, Party – but as the poor men and women who think and act in a present which is always transient and limited; but that same limitation is the condition of our strength – we can be ourselves and regard ourselves as constructors of the world only insofar as the gods have died. There is no longer a logos.
>
> Ernesto Laclau[25]

> Our diversity is a strength: let's value it.
>
> Mobil Corporation advertising logo[26]

Ten years ago such story-telling informed the counter-history undertaken by the influential socialist-feminist text, *Beyond the Fragments*.[27] Taking stock of the uneven development of a dialogue between the male-dominated Left and the 1970s women's liberation movement, it emphasised the important differences between the organisational form of political parties and the participatory politics of movements such as feminism. Sheila Rowbotham's nuanced account of the political culture of sectarianism on the British Left – dominated by macho dogmatism and the authoritative stance of Leninist vanguard leadership – drew attention to the 'emotionally terrorising morality' of being 'politically correct' in order to lay claim to the identity of being a 'true' socialist.[28] Considering the transformative impact of various feminisms over the past two decades, it seems to me that the contrasting decline of the organised Left can be accounted for by just such unpleasant behaviours concerning one's 'correct' credentials. Such attitudes also contribute to the widespread apathy and boredom inspired by conventional

Left/Right politics today. In the wake of heroic models of modernist commitment the withdrawal of affective involvement from formal politics, like the decline of the public sphere itself, underlines postmodern indifference and the privatisation of political passions (the so-called 'crisis of caring') as much as it underpins the rise of 'conviction' politics and all sorts of fundamentalism which speak in the name of the silent majorities.

So where is the passion that was once invested in the Left? Such passion certainly exists, as has been seen in the system of equivalences unfolding in the Communist world as a result of glasnost and perestroika. Gramsci argued for a symbolic view of politics and power as his conception of the party as a 'modern prince' was based on the argument that all forms of living political practice necessarily produce 'myth', which is

> expressed neither in the form of a cold utopia nor as learned theorising, but rather by a creation of concrete phantasy which acts on a dispersed and shattered people to arouse and organise its collective will.[29]

The New Right has certainly heeded such Gramscian advice: since 1968 the 'concrete phantasy' that has aroused and organised the collective will of the British people has been hegemonised and directed by the bifurcated neo-conservative vision of shrinking freedom and deepening inequalities. The myth of a socialist society on the other hand, for so long institutionalised in the image of the 'caring' welfare state, is tattered, torn and untenable. Moreover, the prospects for reconstruction look bleak as the organised Left – what's left of it – has shown no sign of being able to grasp the imaginary and symbolic dimensions of hegemonic strategy. Even when sections of the British Left have mobilised an alternative populism against the Tories, as occurred in the GLC experience (borrowing 'rainbow coalition' imagery from Jesse Jackson's Democratic campaigns in the USA), the 'thinkability' of new alliances has been undermined from within by the conservative traditionalism of the Left, as well as by the essentialist tendencies of 'identity politics' on the part of the new movements.

Since the 1950s, the new social movements have autonomously constructed diverse myths and fantasies which have not only empowered people in their everyday lives, but which have thereby enriched and expanded the horizon of popular politics. But in the plurality of particularisms what can also be seen at the outer limits of the new diversified and decentred public sphere is the paradoxical replication of an authoritarian desire for a centre. The Left's sectarian or doctrinaire anxiety over the 'correct' interpretation of the master-thinkers Marx, Lenin and Trotsky is reproduced at a subjective level in the new movements by the ethical imperative of 'authenticity', expressed in the righteous rhetoric of being 'ideologically right on'. The moral masochism that informs the attitude-policing and credibility-inspection routines so characteristic of the separatist tendencies of some of the autonomous movements reproduces the monologic and puritanical conception of agency found in marxian economism and class essentialism. The search for an authentic, essential 'self' in adversarial ideologies such as black cultural nationalism or lesbian-feminist separatism, to cite just two examples, replays the vanguardist notion that there can be only one privileged agent of social and historical change. However tactically necessary in the 'war of manoeuvre' against white/male supremacist ideologies, the consequences of such separatism is self-defeating as it mimics the authoritarian power to which it is initially opposed by simply inverting the binarism of discourses that legitimate domination. In any case, such fixed beliefs in immutable identity within the new antagonisms of race, gender, ethnicity and sexuality have been called into question by the pluralisation effect that occurs in the encounter between the different movements – something that has become more pronounced in the 1980s. The emergence of black women as a distinct 'class' or group in politics, for example, has relativised radical feminist notions of 'global sisterhood' by raising issues of racial and ethnic oppression that cut across experiences of power and powerlessness among women. By the same logic, black feminist positions disrupt complacent notions of a homogeneous and self-identical 'black community' by highlighting gender antagonisms and the divisive consequences of macho rhetoric in black political strategies.[30]

Essentialist notions of identity and subjectivity surface in the vortex of this bewildering experience of difference because of the absence of a common idea of what diversity really means for the multitude of subjects, actors and agents who are deeply unhappy with and antagonistic towards New Right hegemony. One appreciates the awfulness of this condition (which marks out the historic failure of the Left) by recognising that the only available ideology which has taken diversity seriously is the social-democratic discourse of 'multi-culturalism' which enjoys little credibility among both racists and anti-racists, Left and Right alike. But in so far as the British Left evacuates and abandons the terrain, it is colonised by the Right and monocultural essentialism is mobilised in the defence of 'our way of life' to deny the very existence of diversity and difference.

Beyond the Fragments was influential (and informed the GLC's project of participatory democracy) because it recognised the diverse sources of antagonism in capitalist society: as Hilary Wainwright said, 'it is precisely the connections between these sources of oppression, both through the state and through the organisation of production and culture, that makes a piecemeal solution impossible'.[31] But in the scenario of further fragmentation and de-totalisation that has characterised the 1980s, who really has the confidence to assume that there is such a transcendental realm of the 'beyond'? Shouldn't we begin again by relativising the perspective to examine the contradictions that characterise the complex relations 'between'? This would mean deepening and extending the analysis of the interdependency of culture and politics in the process by which men and women 'acquire consciousness of social relations'. It would also entail a more detailed understanding of the salient differences and similarities between political parties and social movements. Alain Touraine has remarked that 'the labour movement, whose power is frequently invoked to underscore the weakness of the new social movements, is not really a wholly social movement'[32] as it has confined itself to class contradictions at the expense of other social antagonisms that do not arise directly out of the conflict of capital and labour. However, to understand the combined and uneven development of potentially counter-hegemonic forces, it is the very dichotomy between the state and civil society that also needs to be reformulated.

First, because it obscures the double-edged paradox whereby the incorporation and neutralisation of the industrial labour movement (in corporatism, bureaucracy and other forms of political mediation) is paralleled by the cultural appropriation and commodification of the new movements, many of whose radical slogans (such as 'the personal is political') have been hijacked, objectified and sold back to us as an ever-widening range of 'lifestyle' options for those who can afford to pay. Yet, just as the welfare state did deliver limited gains by extending citizenship rights from the legal and political to the social arena, the new movements have had significant impact on personal relations and lived experience precisely through the diffusion of their ideologies in the commodified forms of the cultural marketplace. Second, the concrete problems of political representation that came to light in the GLC experiment demonstrated that the distinction between state formation and the public sphere is not an impassable or absolute boundary, but nevertheless a boundary through which it is difficult simply to translate correspondences from one to the other. Paul Gilroy's reading of the 'success' of the Rock Against Racism campaign in civil society in the 1970s and the 'failure' of top-down bureaucratic methods of municipal anti-racism in the 1980s, highlights the degree of incommensurability between the two.[33] But because the analysis remains within the state/civil society dichotomy it describes, it cannot identify the pragmatic points of entry from which to conduct or prefigure counter-hegemonic strategy 'in and against' the state. Given the legacy of statism within the British labour movement, one cannot simply withdraw from the task of conceptualising the necessary transformation of the state and its role in socialist strategy.

The official discourse of anti-racism failed precisely because it imposed a one-dimensional view of racial antagonism in practices such as 'racism awareness training', which simply reinforced existing relations of minority representation. Problems of tokenism – in which the one black person on the committee or in the organisation is positioned, or rather burdened, with the role of a 'representative' who 'speaks for' the entire community from which she or he comes – were left intact. Black subjects historically marginalised from political representation by exclusionary practices reproduced within the Left were legitimately angry. But the encoding of such anger often took the displaced form of 'guilt-tripping' in which potential allies were paralysed by the sins of their past. White activists recognised the untenable innocence of conciliatory liberal pluralism, but without a common set of terms in which to share openly criticism and disagreements, alliance-building was inhibited by the fear of being seen to be 'incorrect' and not 'ideologically right on'. Rather than learn from the educative value of errors and active mistakes, action was inhibited by a dogmatic discourse of anti-racism which merely disguised the guilt, anger and resentment that gave urgency to issues of race and racism. In my view solidarity does not mean that everyone thinks in the same way, it begins when people have the confidence to disagree over issues of fundamental importance precisely because they 'care' about constructing common ground. It is around such passions encountered in the pluralised and diversified forms of contemporary democracy that the issue of alliances needs to be rethought through an expanded and *modernised* conception of citizenship.

The concept of citizenship is crucial because, in a democracy, it operates in the hinge that articulates civil society and the state in an open-ended or indeterminate relationship. In the modern period, somewhere between 1880 and 1920, the industrial labour movement contested the narrow range of citizenship rights of 'the people' within liberal democracy. The gradual enfranchisement of excluded and marginalised subjects, as the result of class struggles, constituted the form of government defined after 1945 as social democracy. In the post-industrial world however, the democratic image of 'the people' has been radically pluralised and hybridised by the proliferation of new antagonisms and the presence of a diversity of social subjects whose needs and interests can no longer be programmed around the limited citizenship rights inscribed in the welfare state. Yet neo-liberal democracy – the freedom and inequality pursued by the New Right – threatens to erode and reduce even such minimal rights by prioritising the market over the state as the ultimate site upon which basic needs and rights are guaranteed only by individual initiative. As Margaret Thatcher told us, 'there is no such thing as society, only individual men and women and families'.

The prospects for a radical renewal of the 'myth' of a socialist society cannot lie in the revival or recycling of Labourite welfare statism, although the defence of minimal legal, political and social rights to employment, housing, health care, education and freedom of association has never been more necessary than it is now. Is it possible to envisage a minimalist state capable of guaranteeing such basic citizenship rights against the structured inequalities produced by free-market forces? John Keane and others have argued that only a new constitutional settlement around an expanded conception of democratic citizenship can make socialism thinkable again.[34] Some sections of the Left in Britain, like *Marxism Today* magazine, would have us believe that the process of rethinking is already underway. But I have yet to hear the chorus of a genuinely plural discourse of the Left which actually acknowledges the sheer difficulty of living with difference.

The post-imperial decline of British manufacturing was once explained as a consequence of the uniquely British resistance to postwar modernisation. Politically, the British Left still resists and retreats from the democratic task that confronts it, namely to thoroughly modernise its conception of what a socialist society could and should be. To date there has been very little sustained analysis of what went wrong in the GLC, and such 'active forgetting' of course serves the purpose of the Tories quite nicely. If however, as Stuart Hall remarked, the noise produced in its attempt to find new forms of democratic representation and participation 'is the positive sound of a real, as opposed to phoney and pacified, democracy at work ... a positive recognition of the necessary tension between civil society and the state',[35] then instead of withdrawing into quiet conformity, the Left has to recognise that it is being called upon actively to enjoy and encourage such noise if it is to 'arouse and organise' a popular counter-hegemonic conception of radical democracy in a plural society. If this is what 'socialist pluralism in a real democracy will be like', we can't go back to the future, so bring the noise.

Notes

[1] Cited in leaflet by Haringey Black Action, co-organisers of the Smash the Backlash demonstration, 2 May 1987. My thanks to Savi Hensman, Black Lesbian and Gay Centre, London, for access to materials on the 'Positive Images' campaign.
[2] 'Welcome to the Jungle', Guns N' Roses, *Appetite for Destruction*, Geffen Records 1988.

[3] Stuart Hall, 'The Great Moving Right Show' and 'Gramsci and Us', *The Hard Road to Renewal: Thatcherism and the Crisis of the Left*, Verso 1988; see also, Andrew Gamble, *The Free Economy and the Strong State: The Politics of Thatcherism*, Macmillan 1988, and Claus Offe, *Contradictions of the Welfare State*, Hutchinson 1984.

[4] Written by David Bowie (1972), performed by Mott the Hoople, *Mott the Hoople Greatest Hits*, CBS Records 1976.

[5] Jacques Donzelot, 'The Apprehension of Time', in Don Barry and Stephen Muecke (eds), *The Apprehension of Time*, Local Consumption Publications, Sydney 1988.

[6] Lawrence Grossberg, 'It's a Sin: Politics, Post Modernity and the Popular', *It's a Sin*, Power Institute Publications, Sydney 1988, p52.

[7] Cited in Jon Savage, 'Do You Know How to Pony? The Messianic Intensity of the Sixties' (1982), in Angela McRobbie (ed.), *Zoot Suits and Second Hand Dresses: An Anthology of Fashion and Music*, Macmillan 1989, p121.

[8] Stuart Hall, 'Popular Democratic vs. Authoritarian Populism: Two Ways of Taking Democracy Seriously', *The Hard Road to Renewal*, *op.cit.*; the concept of frontier-effects is originally developed in Ernesto Laclau, *Politics and Ideology in Marxist Theory*, Verso 1977.

[9] Dick Hebdige, 'Digging for Britain: An Excavation in 7 Parts', in *The British Edge*, Institute of Contemporary Arts, Boston, 1987.

[10] *Melody Maker*, 19 August 1989.

[11] Judith Williamson, 'The Problem with being Popular', *New Socialist*, September 1986.

[12] Rosalind Coward and John Ellis, *Language and Materialism: Developments in Semiology and the Theory of the Subject*, Routledge 1977.

[13] Stuart Hall, 'The Rediscovery of Ideology: Return of the Repressed in Media Studies', in M. Gurevitch, T. Bennett, J. Curran and S. Woolacott (eds), *Culture, Society and the Media*, Methuen 1982, pp59-62; see also, Stuart Hall, 'New Ethnicities', in Kobena Mercer (ed.), *Black Film/British Cinema*, ICA Document 7, ICA/BFI 1988.

[14] V.N. Volosinov, *Marxism and the Philosophy of Language*, (1929), Harvard 1973.

[15] Stuart Hall, *Ibid*.

[16] Chantal Mouffe and Ernesto Laclau, *Hegemony and Socialist Strategy: Towards a Radical Democratic Politics*, Verso 1985; the riddle comes from a review by Andrew Ross, *m/f*, no. 11/12, 1986.

[17] Chantal Mouffe, 'Hegemony and New Political Subjects: Toward a New Concept of Democracy', in Cary Nelson and Lawrence Grossberg (eds), *Marxism and the Interpretation of Culture*, Macmillan 1988, p100.

[18] Chantal Mouffe, *Ibid*.

[19] Kwame Nkrumah, *I Speak of Freedom: An African Ideology*, Heinemann 1961; Frantz Fanon, *Black Skin, White Mask*, (1952), Pluto 1986.

[20] Manning Marable, *Race, Reform and Rebellion: The Second Reconstruction in Black America, 1945-1982*, Macmillan 1984; see especially Ch.5, 'Black Power, 1965-1970'.

Welcome to the Jungle

[21] The White Panther manifesto, the 'Woodstock Nation' and other documents from the counter-culture in Britain, Europe and the USA are reprinted in Peter Stansill and David Zane Mairowitz (eds), *BAMN (By Any Means Necessary): Outlaw Manifestos and Ephemera, 1965-1970*, Penguin 1971; on the 'alternative society' in Britain see David Widgery, *The Left in Britain, 1956-1968*, Penguin 1976. On feminist and gay equivalences see Robin Morgan, 'Goodbye to All That' (1970) in *BAMN*, op.cit., and Aubrey Walter (ed.), *Come Together: The Years of Gay Liberation, 1970-73*, Gay Mens Press 1980.

[22] *Marxism and the Philosophy of Language, op.cit.*, pp23-24.

[23] Key speeches of the 1960s are reprinted in Enoch Powell, *Freedom and Reality*, Elliot Right Way Books 1969; see also John Elliot, *Powell and the 1970 Election*, Elliot Right Way Books 1970, and Tom Nairn, *The Break-Up of Britain: Crisis and Neo-Nationalism*, Verso 1977, especially Ch.6 'English Nationalism: The Case of Enoch Powell'.

[24] Walter Benjamin, 'Theses on the Philosophy of History' (1940), *Illuminations*, Fontana 1973, p257.

[25] Ernesto Laclau, 'Building a New Left: An Interview', *Strategies*, no.1, Fall 1988, University of California Los Angeles.

[26] Advert in *Black Enterprise* magazine, Jan.-Feb.1989.

[27] Sheila Rowbotham, Lynn Segal, Hilary Wainwright, *Beyond the Fragments: Feminism and the Making of Socialism*, Merlin Press 1979.

[28] Sheila Rowbotham, 'The Women's Movement and Organizing for Socialism', *ibid.*, p126.

[29] Antonio Gramsci, 'The Modern Prince', *Selections from the Prison Notebooks*, Lawrence & Wishart 1971, p126.

[30] See, 'Black Feminist Perspectives', *Feminist Review*, no.17, 1984; Barbara Smith (ed.), *Home Girls: A Black Feminist Anthology*, Kitchen Table Press 1983; Bell Hooks, *Talking Back: Thinking Feminist, Thinking Black*, Sheba Feminist Publishers 1989.

[31] Hilary Wainwright, 'Introduction', *Beyond the Fragments, op.cit.*, p4.

[32] Alain Touraine, *The Return of the Actor: Social Theory in Post-Industrial Society*, University of Minnesota 1988, p131.

[33] Paul Gilroy, *There Ain't No Black in the Union Jack*, Hutchinson 1987, especially Ch.4, 'Two Sides of Anti-Racism', pp 114-152.

[34] John Keane (ed.), *Democracy and Civil Society*, Verso 1988.

[35] Stuart Hall, 'Face the Future', *The Hard Road to Renewal, op.cit.*, p235; see also Franco Bianchini, 'GLC RIP: Cultural Policies in London, 1981-1986', *New Formations*, no.1, Spring 1987, Routledge.

Confinement

FRANCES ANGELA

This work is about my life, about old and new struggles. One of these photographs represents my grandmother, a significant figure in my early life. Others feature my mother, although in some it is difficult to say whether it is her or me. The pictures touch on different themes: childhood, fantasy, sexuality, religion, desire and pleasure, mental illness and class. All these strands have shaped my life, but they cannot be represented separately. They hold meaning over each other and together they articulate my struggles over identity, about this attempt to represent a life on the margins. Just as language is a site of struggle, so too is representation.

These representations span my movement from the margins and into those centred institutions of higher education. They mark that painful attempt to grasp a language and struggle with theories that can explain and articulate my life. In speaking about myself and representing my subjectivities in these pictures I am also representing the experience of many other working-class women. Not only in that struggle to find words but in that very excursion into those places where we have been constructed as the Other, where our very presence and concerns are seen as disruptive.

I have come to believe that my subordinate identity, growing up as a girl on the margins of the working class, defies any ability to move completely beyond it. Casting off the logic of our pasts and histories that runs through our lives is not easily done. Class for me was labour, a lack of social rights and the heavy weight of servility which harnessed me to the whims, desires and uses of others. If I have to think of one word that could work as a motif of this experience it is *confinement* – the shrinking of horizons, the confinements of space, of physical and assertive movements within institutions, the servility that masqueraded as civility, the subjugation of my body, emotions and psyche, the lack of opportunities in employment and education. These are the traces of the past that work, even now, on my mind and body, that have left their marks and scars on my mental and physical health.

When I came to untying the physical and ideological knots that secured my oppression as a working-class woman I hadn't imagined it would be so hard. It was then that I realised I was still living in those old spaces of servility – wanting to please, knowing absolutely my place. My photographs come out of those spaces and begin to tell a story of my silenced past, in which I also was complicit in denying my desire to belong to the centre. They come out of the old sense of powerlessness and they begin to express the pain and cost of that struggle. They make no claim to portraying some truth about my past, no claim to some authentic identity. They suggest movement rather than fixity.

This movement does not abandon that marginal class position; rather, it places me back there no longer servile, no longer confined, nor living with that sense that I've always been cleaning someone else's house. This is a place of resistance, not defined by poverty, deprivation and toil, but a history that is acknowledged, that has a determining effect on personal and political identity. This place is neither the old margin nor the co-option of the centre, but a third space where new subjectivities, new politics and new identities are articulated. My new location has the resources of the centre but remains outside to disrupt and resist, continually threatening the centre with the contradictions of its margins.

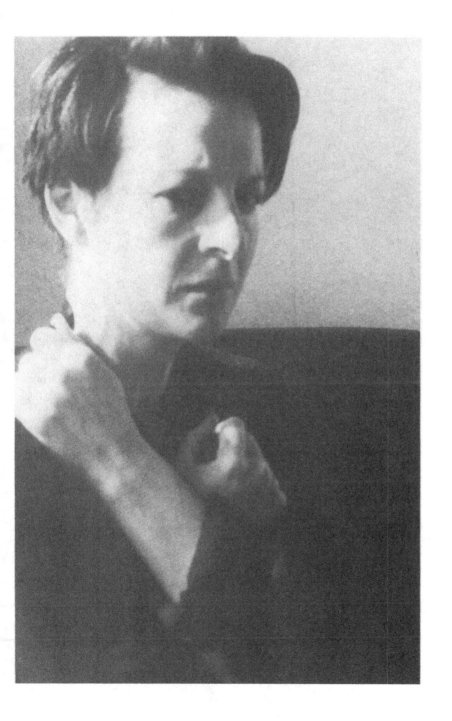

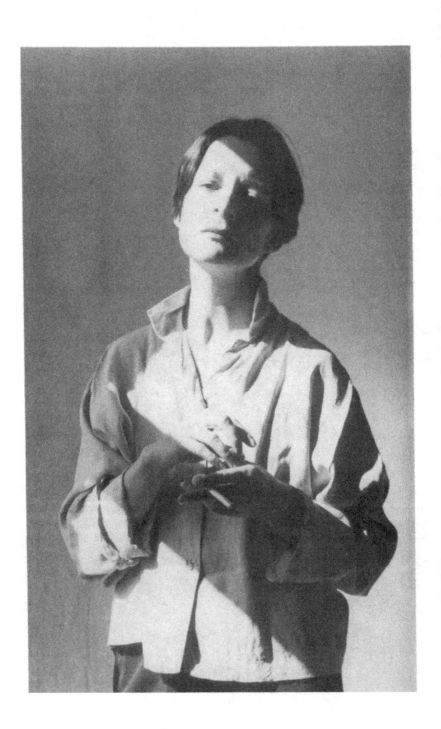

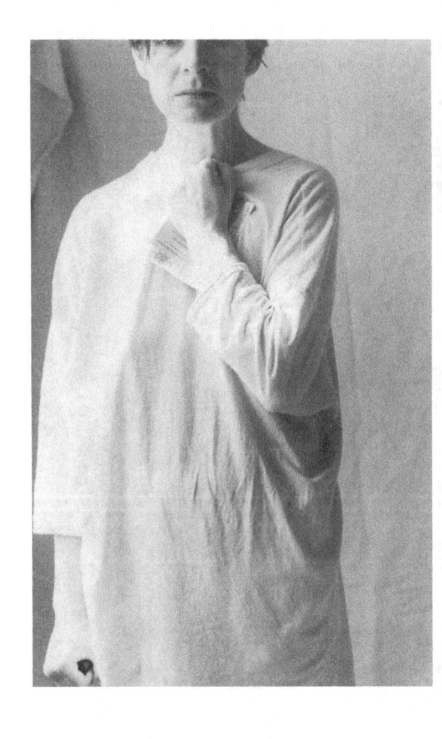

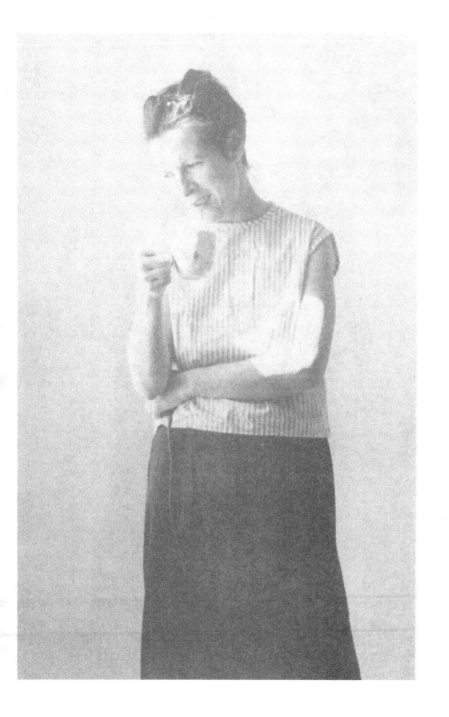

The Value of Difference

JEFFREY WEEKS

A Question of Values

Identity is about belonging, about what you have in common with
some people and what differentiates you from others. At its most
basic it gives you a sense of personal location, the stable core to your
individuality. But it is also about your social relationships, your
complex involvement with others, and in the modern world these
have become ever more complex and confusing. Each of us live with
a variety of potentially contradictory identities, which battle within
us for allegiance: as men or women, black or white, straight or gay,
able-bodied or disabled, 'British' or 'European' ... The list is
potentially infinite, and so therefore are our possible belongings.
Which of them we focus on, bring to the fore, 'identify' with,
depends on a host of factors. At the centre, however, are the values
we share or wish to share with others.

'Identity politics' was initially defined by and for the new social
movements that came to public consciousness from the late 1960s:
the black movement, feminism, lesbian and gay liberation and so on.
The question of integrating these creative but diffuse and potentially
divisive forces into the political mainstream has been part of the
agony of the Left during the last decade. Issues of identity are now,
however, at the centre of modern politics. When Mrs Thatcher
utters anathemas against Brussels and all its works, or interfers in
the details of the history curriculum, she is engaged in an exercise in
delineating a cultural and political identity, in this case of
'Britishness', which she wants us to share. When President
Gorbachev discourses on 'our common European home' he is
striving to re-form our perception of the Soviet identity, and to
re-fashion our idea of Europe. When the Bradford mullahs organise

against *The Satanic Verses* and follow the Ayatollah's *fatwa* they are simultaneously affirming and fashioning an identity – as Muslims, but also as a black British community entitled to the protection of the blasphemy laws like Anglicans and Catholics and evangelicals. When we mourn with students in Beijing, or express solidarity with black South Africans, or run (or sing, or joke) 'for the world', we are striving to realise our identities as members of the global village, as citizens of the world.

Identities are not neutral. Behind the quest for identity are different, and often conflicting values. By saying who we are, we are also striving to express what we are, what we believe and what we desire. The problem is that these beliefs, needs and desires are often patently in conflict, not only between different communities but within individuals themselves.

All this makes debates over values particularly fraught and delicate: they are not simply speculations about the world and our place in it; they touch on fundamental, and deeply felt, issues about who we are and what we want to be and become. They also pose major political questions: how to achieve a reconciliation between our collective needs as human beings and our specific needs as individuals and members of diverse communities, how to balance the universal and the particular. These are not new questions, but they are likely, nevertheless, to loom ever-larger as we engage with the certainty of *un*certainty that characterises 'new times'.

The Return of Values

This is the background to a new concern with values in mainstream politics. Most notoriously, Mrs Thatcher has invoked 'Victorian values' and has pronounced about everything from soccer hooliganism, to religion, to litter. Even the Labour Party, in an uncharacteristic burst of philosophising, has produced a statement on *Democratic Socialist Aims and Values*. And these are but the tips of an iceberg.

Such flurries have not been entirely absent in the past from British political and cultural history. But on the whole, from the Second World War until recently, the political class eschewed too searching a discussion of values, preferring, in Harold Macmillan's

world-weary remark, to leave that to the bishops. During the years
of the social-democratic consensus, welfarism, with its commitment
to altruism and caring, provided a framework for social policy, but
offered little guidance on the purposes of the good society.

Similarly, in the sphere of private life, the most coherent
framework of moral regulation, that enshrined in the 'permissive
reforms' in the 1960s of the laws relating to homosexuality, abortion,
censorship etc, is based on a deliberate suspension of any querying
of what is 'right' or 'wrong'. It relies instead on subtle distinctions
between what the law may accept for public behaviour in upholding
'public decency', and what can be tolerated in private when the
curtains are closed. Most of us are probably quietly grateful for such
small mercies.

As the postwar consensus has crumbled, however, the search for
more or less coherent value-systems has become rather more
fevered. On a personal level some people have moved
promiscuously through drugs and alternative lifestyles to health fads
and religion; a number seek to be 'born again'. Perhaps most of us
just share a vague feeling that things are not quite right. On the level
of politics, various fundamentalisms, on Left and Right, have burst
forth, each articulating their own truth, whether it be about the
perils of pornography, the wrongs done to animals, the rights and
wrongs of this or that religion, or the marvels of the market
economy. There is a new climate where values matter, and
politicians, willy-nilly, are being drawn into the debate.

'Speaking of values', as the philosopher Paul Feyerabend has said,
'is a roundabout way of describing the kind of life one wants to lead
or thinks one wants to lead'.[1] Mrs Thatcher has been clearer about
the sort of life she wants us to lead than any other recent political
leader. She does not trust her bishops, so the values of the
corner-shop and the cautious housewife have expanded inexorably
into the culture of enterprise and the spiritual significance of
capitalism. From her paean to 'Victorian values' in the run-up to the
1983 General Election to her address to the General Assembly of
the Church of Scotland in May 1988, Mrs Thatcher's moral outlook
has had, in Jonathan Raban's phrase, a peculiar 'integrity'.[2]

Questions of value have traditionally been more central to
socialist debates than to conservatism but during the 1970s and early

1980s the nervous collapse of the Left allowed little room for such niceties. Recently, there have been welcome signs of a revival of concern with basic values. The Labour Party's 1988 statement, *Democratic Socialist Aims and Values*, intended to frame the party's policy review, may have been too bland for many people's taste ('The true purpose of democratic socialism ... is the creation of a genuinely free society') but it was the first time since 1917 that the Party had attempted to define its purposes, and in a recognisable philosophical tradition (essentially the rights based liberalism of the American philosopher, John Rawls).

At the same time the Party seems to be attempting to resurrect the half-buried collectivist traditions of the British population. The lyrical Kinnock election broadcast in 1987 subliminally told us of the importance of rootedness and belonging as the basis for political advance. The Labour Party's poster campaign early in 1989 – 'The Labour Party. *Our* party' – similarly articulated a sense of shared values, of communal spirit, lying latent in the collective unconscious.

In part, of course, these Labour Party innovations illustrate the wizardry of ad-agency skills, but it is not too fanciful to see them as a reflection of broader tendencies towards reasserting universal humanistic values, which transcend conventional political divisions. In their different ways, President Gorbachev and green politics have made an impact because of their expression of a human solidarity underlying the divisions of the world. Gorbachev's address to the United Nations in 1988 turned on a call to respect 'universal human values', and looked forward to an ending of the arbitrary divisions between peoples. Green philosophy calls on the same sense of our common destiny and interdependence, as human beings and as fellow inhabitants of spaceship earth, and in doing so claims to displace traditional divisions between Left and Right.

It is impossible to underestimate the power of these various (and perhaps sometimes contradictory) appeals to human solidarity after a decade dominated by an ethic of human selfishness. We are reminded that what we have in common as human beings is more important than what divides us as individuals or members of other collectivities.

Difference

Nevertheless there are difficulties for the Left in an all-embracing humanism. As a philosophical position it may be a good starting point, but it does not readily tell us how to deal with difference. As President Gorbachev could bitterly affirm, it is difference – economic, national, linguistic, ethnic, religious – and the conflicting identities and demands that diversity gives rise to, that poses a major threat to perestroika, and to human solidarity. If ever-growing social complexity, cultural diversity and a proliferation of identities are indeed a mark of the postmodern world, then all the appeals to our common interest as humans will be as naught unless we can at the same time learn to live with difference. This should be the crux of modern debates over values.

In confronting the challenge of social and moral diversity, the responses of Left and Right are significantly different. The Right has a coherent, if in the long run untenable, view of the moral economy. At its most extreme, expressed in Mrs Thatcher's dictum that there is no such thing as society, only individuals and their families, difference becomes merely a matter of individual quirks or pathologies. Social goods are products of individual wills or desires, mediated by family responsibilities. In the economic sphere, this leads to a privileging of individual choice, 'the essence' – as Mrs Thatcher put it during the 1987 election campaign – of morality. But moral choice, in turn, particularly with regard to issues such as sexuality, is limited by the commitment to a traditional concept of domestic obligation, in and through the family.

The Left, on the other hand, is heir to a strong sense of collective identities, of powerful inherited solidarities derived from class and work communities, and of different social constituencies, however inadequately in the past it has been able to deal with them. Multi-culturalism, as it was articulated from the 1960s in the legislation on racial equality, embodied a notion of different communities evolving gradually into a harmonious society where difference was both acknowledged and irrelevant. In rather less hopeful times, the commitment to the co-existence of different value-systems is implied in the statement on *Democratic Socialist Aims and Values*: 'Socialists rejoice in human diversity'.[3] But the

Left has been less confident and sure-footed when faced by the reality of difference.

When the Livingstone-led Greater London Council attempted to let a hundred flowers bloom at County Hall in pursuit of a new majority of minorities, the response of the Labour Party establishment varied from the sceptical to the horrified. Nor should we be entirely surprised at that: despite its political daring, and commendable commitment to those hitherto excluded from the political mainstream, it was difficult to detect behind the GLC policy anything more coherent than the belief that grass-roots activity and difference in itself were prime goods. 'Empowerment', yes; but whom should the Left empower?

The Salman Rushdie crisis has dramatised the absence of any clear-cut philosophy on the Left. The Rushdie affair is important for socialists not simply because it concerns the fate of an individual (and an individual of the Left at that) but because it underscores in the most painful way the dilemmas of diversity. At its simplest we have an apparent conflict of absolutes: the right of an author to freedom of speech, to challenge whomsoever he wishes in a democratic society, set against the claims of a distinctive moral community not to have its fundamental religious beliefs attacked and undermined. But of course the real divisions are more complex and profound.

The Left has not on the whole been willing to endorse an absolute right of free speech. On the contrary it has supported campaigns against racist and sexist literature, whilst a strong minority has supported the banning of pornography. On the other side, the Muslim communities at the centre of the crisis are themselves not monolithic, bisected as they inevitably are by antagonisms of class and gender, and by political conflicts. At the same time the issues raised do not exist only in a meta-realm of principle: they work their way through the murky world of politics, in this case the complexities of international politics as well as the ward by ward, constituency by constituency problems of Labour politicians.

Nevertheless, there is a central question at the heart of the Rushdie affair, and it concerns the possibilities and limits of pluralism in a complex society. Let's take as an example the question of religious education in schools: the government by insisting under the 1988 Education Reform Act that there should be a daily act of Christian worship in maintained schools is in effect asserting the centrality of the Christian tradition to, in Mrs Thatcher's words, 'our national heritage' – 'For centuries it has been our very life-blood'. People with other faiths and cultures are always, of course, welcome in '*our* land', but their beliefs can only, by implication, ever hope to have a secondary position in relation to 'ours'.[4]

Labour, however, accepts a less monolithic view of our religious past and present. As a result it seems prepared to support the principle of state-funding of separate 'fundamentalist' Muslim schools. There is a certain multi-cultural rationale in this: if Anglican, Jewish and Roman Catholic schools are supported by the state, there seems no logic in not supporting the schools of other faiths as well. But schools transmit cultural values, some of which in the case of fundamentalists run counter to oft-declared values of the Left. In this case, the schools will be based on a principle of sex-segregation which elsewhere Labour opposes. As a letter to the *Guardian* from Southall Black Sisters put it, 'the Labour Party is prepared to abandon the principle of equality where black women are concerned. Instead, they deliver us into the hands of male, conservative and religious forces within our communities, who deny us our right to live as we please'.[5] This underlines the danger of seeing communities as unified wholes, rather than as the locus of debate and divisions. Not surprisingly, the 'multi-culturalist' values of the Labour Party seem as likely to cause confusion, conflict and distrust as the explicitly mono-culturalist views of the Right.

It is ironically appropriate that these dilemmas should have been brought to the surface by the publication of, and reaction to, Rushdie's *The Satanic Verses*. Not only was the book written by an 'immigrant' and about 'immigrants', but the book itself, as Malise Ruthven argued on its publication, is about 'changing identities', about the transformations of identities that affect migrants who leave the familiar reference points of their homeland and find themselves in a place where the rules are different, and all the markers have been changed.[6] This is not simply the experience of the migrant: the sense of dislocation and disorientation, of the rules of the game subtly changing, of the co-existence within us of conflicting needs, desires and identities, is becoming a major cultural experience for us all.

Choice

The basic issue can be stated quite simply: by what criteria can we choose between the conflicting claims of different loyalties? To ask the question immediately underlines the poverty of our thinking about this. Can the 'rights' of a group obliterate the 'rights' of an individual? Should the morality of one sector of the population be allowed to limit the freedom of other citizens. To what extent should one particular definition of the good and the just prevail over others? These are ancient questions, but the alarming fact is that the Left lacks a common language for addressing them, let alone resolving them.

There have been two characteristic approaches on the Left in confronting these dilemmas. Firstly, there is the 'discourse of rights', probably still the most potent mobilising force in the worlds of politics and morality. In the United States the protection of individual rights is enshrined in the constitution, and the claim to group rights has become the basis of many of the transforming currents of recent American politics, from the civil rights and black power movements to the women's movement and lesbian and gay liberation. Elsewhere in the West, a rights-based politics is similarly enshrined in written constitutions, bills of rights, constitutional courts, and so on.

In Britain, the tradition is enfeebled. Individual rights, though much bandied around in the political rough and tumble, are not entrenched in a constitutional settlement, and the concept of group rights barely exists. Rights are, however, clearly back on the agenda of the Left: the response to the launch of Charter 88, with its appeal for a new constitutional settlement, with government subordinate to the law and basic rights guaranteed, suggests there is a strongly felt need for a codification and protection of fundamental rights.

Unfortunately, the claim to right, however well established at a constitutional level, does not help when rights are seen to be in conflict. To take the issue of abortion (yet again the focus of moral debate in America and Britain), here the conflict is between two violently conflicting claims to right: the rights of the 'unborn child' against the rights of a woman to control her own body. In these stark terms the conflict is unresolvable, because two value-systems tug in

95

quite different directions. The problem is that rights do not spring fully armed from nature. They cannot find a justification simply because they are claimed. Rights are products of human association, social organisation, traditions of struggle, and historical definitions of needs and obligations: whatever their claims to universality, they are limited by the philosophical system to which they belong, and the social and political context in which they are asserted. This is not to deny the importance of rights-based arguments. But if we are to take rights seriously we must begin to articulate the sort of rights and the type of political culture we want.[7]

This is the starting point for the second major approach to the dilemma of choice, the politics of emancipation. In his essay 'On the Jewish Question' in the 1840s Marx counterposed to the 'morality of Rights' a 'morality of emancipation', and even more powerfully than the claim to rights this has proved a potent mobilising force.[8] It offers a vision of a totally free society, where everyone's potentiality is fully realised, and a powerful analysis of the constraints on the realisation of human emancipation. At its heart is a denial that want, division, selfishness and conflict are essential parts of human nature. True human nature, it claims, can flourish in a truly emancipated society.

Most of us who are socialist must have been inspired by this vision. As a politics of liberation it shaped the rhetoric of the social movements that emerged in the 1960s. It is still latent in the hunger for utopia and for the transcendence of difference that shades our politics. The difficulty is that the practice has rarely kept up with the vision, particularly in the history of Marxism. The Marxist tradition has been reluctant to define the nature of the emancipated society, and has been noticeably blind to questions of nationalism, ethnicity, gender and sexuality. Nor do the experiences of the *soi disant* socialist countries offer much confidence in the attainability of emancipation in the terms offered by the tradition so far.

We must not confuse a noble goal with the sordid practices of particular regimes, but we need to ponder whether the very project of human emancipation as conventionally set forth is not itself the fundamental problem. The glorious goal has all too often justified dubious means, whilst the absence of any detailed exposition of the meaning of emancipation has left us floundering when faced by the reality of conflicting claims to right and justice.

Radical Pluralism

The Rushdie affair has underlined the inadequacy of the existing languages of rights and emancipation for dealing with real conflicts. Rights-based arguments leave us staring blankly at conflicting claims, while an emancipatory rhetoric leaves Rushdie trapped in his safe-house. In practice, in the absence of anything better we seem to be faced by two stark alternatives. On the one hand we have a call to respect absolutely the rights of a specific community to organise its own way of life, regardless of the traditions of the wider community as a whole. This has been put most clearly by Keith Vaz MP: 'To goad and mock the new religions is to rob them of their roots and sensitivities. They must be left to develop in their own way'.[9] This in effect is an appeal to give full play to cultural difference, whatever the implications, simply because enough people are willing and able to affirm the importance of what is different. On the other hand, there is a despair of the challenge of diversity. The novelist Fay Weldon has put it sharply: 'Our attempt at multi-culturalism has failed ... The uniculturalist policy of the United States *worked*, welding its new peoples, from every race, every belief, into a whole'.[10] Pluralism is in fact institutionalised rather than obliterated in the USA, and intercommunal strife is not exactly unknown. But the philsophy of assimilation, where differences dissolve in the great 'melting pot' of America, obviously still has a powerful appeal.

Neither position really deals with the fundamental issues. One in effect insists that it is impossible to evaluate different traditions. The other hopes that the claims of other traditions may dissolve into a greater whole. These opposed positions are effectively mirror-images of each other, both assuming that differences must be absolute. The reality is much more contradictory. Different identities, and the social solidarities that sustain them, reflect the variety of individual and social needs in the modern world. Such needs are in constant flux, and change over time. They cannot be frozen by any moral system; indeed, the fervour and anger of fundamentalism can be seen as a reflex against the rapidity of change, where everything that was fixed begins to seem radically uncertain. To be able to deal with the world as it is, and to change it, we need a language of politics that is able to speak to difference and uncertainty within a framework of common principles.

There is no ready-made blueprint for this but as a first step we could usefully learn the value of what Feyerabend calls a 'democratic relativism',[11] which recognises that there are many different ways of being and many truths in the world; people should have a right to live in the ways that satisfy their needs.

In the Rushdie case, this implies respect for the traditions and aspirations of the Muslim community, and the creation of protected spaces where their voices may be heard. But radical relativism can only work if arguments over needs can be conducted freely and democratically in each community, and between different communities. Communities of identity are never monolithic: they embody traditions of arguments and debate, as the feminist interventions within the Muslim community illustrate. We need a democratic framework which allows debate to flourish.

So the recognition of a plurality of truths is a starting point only. It in turn must be governed by what David Held has called the principle of democratic autonomy.[12] This argues that citizens should be free and equal in the determination of the conditions of their own lives, sharing equal rights and obligations, so long as they do not use their freedoms to negate the rights and claims of others. Democratic autonomy implies a respect and tolerance for other people's needs as the guarantee of your own freedom to choose. Groups and communities become potentially undemocratic, as fundamentalists of whatever flavour do, when they begin to proclaim the universal truth of their particular experiences. The freedom to live your own life in the way you choose must imply an acceptance of other ways of life. Rushdie has found to his cost that this principle as yet has very little leverage in the fundamentalist community he was addressing.

Such principles, simple to write, painful to live, imply the existence of a wider political community based on acceptance of diversity and democracy. We may not be able to find, indeed we should not seek, a single way of life that would satisfy us all. That does not mean we cannot agree on common political ends: the construction of what can best be described as 'a community of communities', to achieve a maximum political unity without denying difference.

Such a political community will necessarily embody a notion of the common good and of justice, in order to regulate the variety of rights and demands. We can list, as socialists have always done, the goals of a just society: the ending of economic exploitation, social inequality, racism, gender and sexual oppression and all the other relations of domination and subordination that inhibit human potentials. But if the desirable ends are not to be undermined, we must pay more attention than many socialists have been willing to do in the past to the means: the development of a polity where differences can be aired and negotiated, and unavoidable conflicts mediated, in a democratic fashion.

These principles are not new. In essence they can be traced back to the earliest discussions of democracy in ancient Greece, and to the ideals of localised democracies of the early American republic. They represent a revitalisation of the communitarian tradition of politics and of a 'civic republicanism'.[13] At the same time they build on those elements of the British socialist tradition which have always stressed the importance of grass-roots activity and democratic control of social and economic life, supported feminist struggles and advocated sexual freedom. 'Radical pluralism' as outlined here is congruent with the best in the democratic and socialist traditions.

This approach to socialist values is at best a framework within which we can begin to rethink the question of difference at both the individual and collective level. Rather more effectively than a simple claim to right, such a position offers a set of criteria for assessing conflicting claims. More modestly than a morality of emancipation it avoids declarations about a final resolution of all conflict in a magical escape from oppression and exploitation. The aim instead is to offer a concept of politics as a process of continuous debate and mutual education, and to broaden the democratic imagination through the acceptance of human variety and difference.

Notes

[1] Paul Feyerabend, *Farewell to Reason*, Verso 1987, p54.

[2] Jonathan Raban, *God, Man and Mrs Thatcher*, Chatto 1989.

[3] The Labour Party, *Democratic Socialist Aims and Values*, London 1988, p7.

[4] The quotations are from Mrs Thatcher's speech to the General Assembly of the Church of Scotland, quoted in Raban, *God, Man and Mrs Thatcher, op.cit.*

[5] *Guardian*, 22 July 1989.

[6] Malise Ruthven, 'A Question of Identity', in Lisa Appignanesi and Sara Maitland (eds), *The Rushdie File*, Fourth Estate 1989, pp21-22.

[7] Steven Lukes, *Marxism and Morality*, Oxford University Press 1985, pp64-65.

[8] *Ibid.* pp27-28.

[9] *Independent*, 29 July 1989.

[10] Fay Weldon, *Sacred Cows*, Chatto 1989, pp31-32.

[11] Feyerabend, *op.cit.*, p54.

[12] David Held, *Models of Democracy*, Polity Press 1987.

[13] See Chantal Mouffe, 'The Civics Lesson', *New Statesman and Society*, 7 October 1988.

Black Feminism: The Politics of Articulation

PRATIBHA PARMAR

Introduction

Black British women are part of many diasporas. All aspects of our photographic, literary and visual representation are organically informed by and shaped through our historical memories and the raw cultural signs and processes of our subjectivities as black British. The richness and complexity of the black cultural 'explosion' has challenged any simple notion of 'identity politics'. It has pointed to the disintegration of that paradigm of identity politics which posits our 'otherness' and 'difference' as singular, seemingly static identities of sexuality, race and gender (with a crude acknowledgement of our disadvantaged economic position).

The photographic work by black women has been a significant part of emergent black cultural practice. It has sought to rework and reinscribe the language and conventions of representation, not simply to articulate our cultural difference, but to strive beyond this and develop a narrative that is wholly encased within our own terms of reference. This entails creating identities as black British women not 'in relation to', 'in opposition to', 'as reversal of', or 'as a corrective to' ... but *in and for ourselves*. Such a narrative thwarts that binary hierarchy of centre and margin: the margin refuses its place as 'Other'.

June Jordan's insight that identities are not fixed but always in a state of flux and change has challenged the desirability of simplistic representations (the notion of positive/negative images) and fixed hierarchies of oppression. On the other hand, we should not regard the terms of our self-definition purely as a matter of individual free choice. What is evident in the cultural productions of black women's creativity is the active negotiation between these objective notions of ourselves (as female, black, lesbian or working-class) and the subjective experiences of displacement, alienation and 'otherness'. The marginal ceases to be the *object* of interpretation and illumination: in our own self-referencing narratives we expropriate those bodies of knowledge and theory which are ethnocentrically bound in a relation of dominance to us as post-colonial subjects.

Both these pieces of writing are my tentative explorations into the politics of location, in order to address first black and migrant women's attempts to secure an authentic visual language, and second the emergence of difference within black feminism. It has been a time for reassessment and critical self-evaluation. While the articulation of self-identities has been a necessary and essential process for collective organising by black and migrant women, it also resulted in political practices which became insular and often retrograde.

Writing has meant exposing myself, as well grappling with theories that might enable a different kind of political discourse of identity; it has meant engaging critically with the categories of self-enunciation which many of us, as activists and theorists in the black women's movement of the late 1970s and early 1980s, had employed. Then I spoke and wrote from a position of marginality and resistance, but always strengthened by the collective consciousness of ourselves as black women, as feminists and as lesbians (albeit a visibly small minority). Today, at the beginning of a new decade I still inhabit that position of marginality and resistance but in the absence of that collective force which momentarily empowered many of us and gave us the 'power of speech'. 'Other Kinds of Dreams' is an optimistic reassessment – coming-to-terms with historical and political realities.

OTHER KINDS OF DREAMS

In 1984 a group of us who guest-edited a special issue of *Feminist Review* entitled 'Many Voices, One Chant: Black Feminist Perspectives' stated in our editorial: 'We have attempted to provide a collection of perspectives which are in the process of continual development, refinement and growth. It [the issue] also indicated some of the diversities within Black feminism, a diversity from which we draw strength.'[1]

Rereading that issue now, four years later, it seems difficult to fathom where the optimism and stridency which many of us had who were active in the black women's movement has gone, and why. Where are the diverse black feminist perspectives which we felt were in the process of growth? And where indeed is the movement itself? In moments of despair one wonders if those years were merely imagined. Four years is not a long time, but it is obviously long enough to see the disintegration of what was once an energetic and active black women's movement: a movement which was given a shape and form by the Organisation of Women of African and Asian Descent (OWAAD) from the late 1970s to the early 1980s. The history of OWAAD and its subsequent demise has been well documented and discussed, for instance by the Brixton Black Women's Group in their article 'Black Women Organising'[2] but suffice it to say here that there were some very real grounds for the optimism that many of us felt as we witnessed and became part of the growth of black women's groups around the country; groups that initiated campaigns around education, housing, immigration, health and policing.

The end of the 1970s saw the demise and fragmentation of the white women's movement and by 1980 the countless campaigns, groups and support networks that had been built up in the 1970s and which were the backbone of the women's movement were already in disarray, as Lynne Segal chronicles so clearly in her book, *Is the Future Female?*[3] Many of these groups and centres re-emerged temporarily through the efforts of municipal feminism whose primary impact was felt throughout the short but vibrant life of the Greater London Council and subsequently on some of the Labour-controlled local authorities. So while the women's movement as a whole was collapsing as a political force and forum, black women were concentrating their energies on building a black women's movement. The brunt of the emerging 'new racism' was being felt keenly by the black communities and by black women in particular. Black women were busy campaigning and creating autonomous organisational structures through our new-found collective self-confidence.

Identity

There is no doubt about the dynamic effects that the black women's movement and black feminism has had, not only on the lives of black women but also on the Women's Liberation Movement and on other progressive movements. One of the challenges that black feminism posed was to the eurocentric theories and practices of white feminism. The take-up of this challenge was very slow, indeed sometimes defensive and racist: for instance, Kum-Kum Bhavnani and I wrote a tentative article for discussion on 'Racism and the Women's Movement' for a workshop on Women Against Racism and Fascism at the 1978 Socialist-Feminist conference. We stated:

> The Women's movement in Britain has never taken up the question of racism in any real way and because this issue affects all black women, we feel that a failure to take it up has ensured and will continue to ensure that the Women's Liberation Movement as a whole is irrelevant to the needs and demands of most black women. It is fairly clear that we are not 'all sisters together' and it is important to understand why this is so. The failure to take this issue seriously has produced certain anomalies in the relationship of feminism to black women and their specific situations.

We then went on to outline and critique feminist analyses and practices around the family, immigration controls, abortion and contraception, and 'reclaim the night' marches.

At the suggestion of the women in the workshop, we sent the article to *Spare Rib*, asking them to publish it in their forum page, which at the time was used to debate issues of pertinence to the women's movement. We received a three-page letter from a member of the collective who attempted to answer our critique: 'The problem is that while *our movement* [my emphasis] is undoubtedly failing to reach large numbers of black women we have not in fact made the precise mistakes your paper describes.' Throughout, she addressed us as if we were speaking from outside of the movement and used 'we' to denote white women as being representative of the women's movement. The letter concluded by stating: 'we didn't really feel your article could form a basis for discussion inside the feminist community as it betrays so many misconceptions about the movement's history.'

Black Feminism: the Politics of Articulation

I quote this incident at length partly to illustrate that it was experiences such as these which made many of us look elsewhere, in particular to other black women, for collective strength, and partly to locate subsequent challenges historically. Since the late 1970s black women have written many articles and books, and organised autonomous publishing resources. This has meant that we are no longer at the mercy of individuals and collectives who censor our work because they disagree with it or find it uncomfortably close to the truth. The theoretical development of a critique of white feminist theories was initiated by Hazel Carby in her article, 'White Women Listen! Black Feminism and the Boundaries of Sisterhood'[4] Subsequently, other articles appeared, including 'Black Feminism: Shared Oppression, New Expression',[5] 'Many Voices, One Chant'[6] and, more recently, the publication of an anthalogy, *Charting the Journey: Writings by Black and Third World Women*.[7] As a result, there has been, albeit belatedly, a certain amount of rethinking among some white socialist feminists, taking up some of the issues black feminists have raised. For instance, 'Many Voices, One Chant' provoked an article by Michèle Barrett and Mary McIntosh entitled, 'Ethnocentrism and Socialist-Feminist Theory'[8] which in turn rekindled the debate on racism and the women's movement.[9]

For me, while there are several problems with some of the critiques and responses that have emerged in recent years to this debate on the challenge of black feminism to white feminist theories, the most important point has been that at least and at last white socialist-feminists are beginning to rethink their positions. But it is not only white socialist-feminists who are rethinking.

Critical self-evaluation is a necessary prerequisite for *all of us* engaged in political struggle if there is to be any movement away from intransigent political positions to tentative new formulations, and such self-evaluation has already begun among some black women. In the preface to *Charting the Journey*, the editors ask:

> For where are we at present? Instead of at least the semblance of a Black women's movement, the futile 'politics' of victim and guilt tripping runs rampant and is used to justify actions that any self-respect would deem impossible. Or there is the tendency towards the collective adornment of moral and political superiority which is supposed to derive from the mere fact of being a Black woman. That this is so gives rise at least to a

105

wistful sigh and more often to a scream from the far reaches of the soul – the only way to express one's disbelief and bewilderment that we could have got here from there.[10]

This article is not an attempt to bemoan the past nor to wring my ands in angst at what went wrong. But it is almost a truism in these mes of reassessment to state that in order to move forward one eeds to learn from the lessons of history. It is not my intention here provide a detailed analysis or assessment of the past and current ate of black women's politics. What follows is a number of initial d exploratory thoughts which have emerged out of discussions ith friends and fellow activists; discussions which have focused on w to move out of the political and theoretical paralysis that seems prevail.

lentity Politics

these postmodernist times the question of identity has taken on lossal weight particularly for those of us who are post-colonial igrants inhabiting histories of diaspora. Being cast into the role of e Other, marginalised, discriminated against and too often visible, not only within everyday discourses of affirmation but also ithin the 'grand narratives' of European thought, black women in articular have fought to assert privately and publicly our sense of lf: a self that is rooted in particular histories, cultures and nguages. Black feminism has provided a space and a framework for e articulation of our diverse identities as black women from fferent ethnicities, classes and sexualities, even though at times at space had to be fought for and negotiated.

To assert an individual and collective identity as black women has en a necessary historical process which was both empowering and rengthening. To organise self-consciously as black women was and ntinues to be important; that form of organisation is not arbitrary, it is based on a political analysis of our common economic, social d cultural oppressions. It is also based on an assumption of shared bjectivities, of the ways in which our experiences of the world 'out ere' are shaped by common objective factors such as racism and xual exploitation.

However, these assumptions have led to a political practice which employs a language of 'authentic subjective experience'. The implications of such a practice are multifold. It has given rise to a self-righteous assertion that if one inhabits a certain identity this gives one the legitimate and moral right to guilt-trip others into particular ways of behaving. The women's movement in general has become dominated by such tendencies. There has been an emphasis on accumulating a collection of oppressed identities which in turn have given rise to a hierarchy of oppression. Such scaling has not only been destructive, but divisive and immobilising. Unwilling to work across all our differences, many women have retreated into ghettoised 'lifestyle politics' and find themselves unable to move beyond personal and individual experience.

Identity politics or a political practice which takes as its starting point only the personal and experiential modes of being has led to a closure which is both retrogressive and sometimes spine-chilling. Take for instance, the example of an article that appeared in *Spare Rib* entitled 'Ten Points for White Women to Feel Guilty About'. The title alone made some of us cringe in despair and consternation. There is an inherent essentialism in such articulations which has become pervasive within the women's movement in general and has led to political fragmentation. Lynne Segal has convincingly critiqued the biologistic and essentialist thinking which has begun to dominate much feminist analysis and practice in the 1980s and I would agree with the conclusion that 'Whereas the problem for women's liberation was once how to assert personal issues as political, the problem has now reversed to one where feminists need to argue that the political does not reduce to the personal'.[11]

Racial Identities

Another problem that has been more specific to black women and the black communities is that of shifting definitions of black identity. While I do want to point to some of the problems and consequences of identity politics I would not want to conclude that any analysis of the political and cultural articulations around identity should be abandoned. Rather, as Stuart Hall has argued:

> It seems to me that it is possible to think about the nature of new political identities, which isn't founded on the notion of some absolute,

integral self and which clearly can't arise from some fully closed narrative of the self. A politics which accepts the 'no necessary or essential correspondence' of anything with anything, and there has to be *a politics of articulation* – politics as a hegemonic project.[12]

ι trying to find my way towards such a politics I myself have turned ι the writings of June Jordan, a black American poet and essayist[13] hose work has clarified many of my doubts and confusions and elped to clear the cobwebs of depair and anger. Val Amos and I ιund her book *Civil Wars* invaluable when we taught an adult ducation class on 'Women and Racism' at London University in 984. At a time when many contemporary movements need to ιassess the method and basis of their organising, June Jordan's ιoral and political vision offers an inspiration. Her commitment to ιternationalism and her ability to articulate the complex links and ιntradictions between the deeply personal and the deeply political ι a clear and passionate way is rare. Her writings are a timely ιminder that identity politics 'may be enough to get started on but ot enough to get anything finished.' She visited Britain for the first me in September 1987 when I talked to her about some of the roblems I have outlined above. Below are extracts from this ιterview by way of a conclusion.[14]

ratibha: One of the most interesting and challenging things I have ιund in your writings is the way in which your radicalism refuses to ιppress the complexity of our identities as women and as black eople. In Britain there has been a tendency in the women's ιovement, both black and white, to organise around the ssumptions of our shared identities but in the process of political rganising many of these assumptions have fallen apart. Can you talk bout some of the issues raised around identity politics and what you ιink it means to define oneself as a political person.

une Jordan: We have been organising on the basis of identity, round immutable attributes of gender, race and class for a long time nd it doesn't seem to have worked. There are obvious reasons for etting together with other people because someone else is black or he is a woman but I think we have to try to develop habits of evaluation in whatever we attempt politically. People get set into certain ways of doing things and they don't evaluate whether it's working or not. Or if they do evaluate then it's to say it's not working but it's not our fault, there couldn't possibly be anything wrong with our thinking on this subject or the issue. The problem invariably is that the enemy is simply inflexible or impregnable. This is a doomed *modus operandi*. We have to find out what works and some things may work to a certain extent and not beyond that.

I don't think that gender politics or that race politics *per se* are isolated from other ways of organising for change, whether reformist change or revolutionary change. I don't think that they will take us where we want to go. I think that's abundantly clear if we look at our history as black people. We as black people have enormous problems everywhere in the world and we women have colossal problems everywhere in the world. I think there is something deficient in the thinking on the part of anybody who proposes either gender identity politics or race identity politics as sufficient, because every single one of us is more than whatever race we represent or embody and more than whatever gender category we fall into. We have other kinds of allegiances, other kinds of dreams that have nothing to do with whether we are white or not white.

A lot of awareness of ourselves as women, as black people and Third World people really comes out of our involuntary forced relationships with people who despise us on the basis of what we are rather than what we do. In other words our political awareness of ourselves derives more often than not from a necessity to find out why it is that this particular kind of persecution continues either for my people, or myself or my kind. Once you try to answer that question you find yourself in the territory of people who despise you, people who are responsible for the invention of the term racism or sexism. I think it's important to understand that each one of us is more than what cannot be changed about us. That seems self-evident and accordingly our politics should reflect that understanding.

This is not at all to disparage or dismiss the necessity for what I would call issue-oriented unity among different kinds of people, women, black people, or black women. I am not dismissing it but just saying that it's probably not enough. It may be enough to get started on something but I doubt very much whether it's enough to get anything finished.

Pratibha: So you are saying that in order to move forward, a crucial part of the political process is to go beyond the personal and experiential ways of organising. You have written, 'It occurs to me that much organisational grief could be avoided if people understood that partnership in misery does not necessarily provide for partnership for change: *when we get the monsters off our backs all of us may want to run in very different directions.'*

June Jordan: Yes, for example, I think that for any woman who has ever been raped, the existence of feminist or all-female rape counselling centres is absolutely necessary, the recourse to a refuge where a woman can retire to repair herself without fear. But the problem is more than an individual problem. She didn't rape herself. In order to eliminate the possibility of rape or even the likelihood of rape for women generally we have to go beyond ourselves. We have to sit down with and/or stand up to and finally in some way impact upon men. I don't think it's ever enough on your own. And I would say the same thing about race identity politics. I didn't, nor did my people or my parents, invent the problems that we as black people have to solve. We black people, the victims of racism are not the ones that have to learn new ways of thinking about things so that we can stop racist habits of thought. Neither do we have the power to be placed in appropriate situations to abolish the social and economic arrangements that have assured the continuity of racism in our lives. That's for white people. What we really need to do is pass the taking of succour from each other, so to speak, and build on our collective confidence and pride. Some people who I have met since I have been in London have been saying, it's terrible because nothing is going on politically. But that's not the point. I don't mean to knock that at all, but okay, now you know and I know that something is terrible, what are you going to do about it. Let's not sit inside our sorrows, let's not describe things to death. My orientation is activism. Other than that's its like a kind of vanity or a decadence. I will tell you how I suffer and you tell me how you suffer ... it's bad enough to suffer but to talk about it endlessly ... I say to them stop it ... stop it ...

Pratibha: Many movements such as the women's movement, the black movement and black women's groups have been organising for a number of years around their shared oppressions. But it seems to me that many of these movements are stagnating because there is a refusal to acknowledge the need to move away from modes of being, that is accumulating all the 'isms' of race, sex, class, disability etc, to modes of doing. What do you think are the dangers of this? How do you think we can move forward from this paralysis.

June Jordan: I am sure there is a danger. The first part of the political process is to recognise that there is a political problem and then to find people who agree with you. But the last part of the political process which is to get rid of it is necessary and something too many of us forget. I am not interested in struggle, I am interested in victory. Let's get rid of the problems, let's not just sit around and talk about it and hold each other's hands. That's where you make the evaluation: is it getting us there? If it's not, then let's have other kinds of meetings with other kinds of people. I think people can get stuck absolutely. What is the purpose of your identity? That is the question. 'So what?' is the way I would put it in my abrupt American way. What do you want to do on the basis of that? You just think that if you fill a room by putting out flyers, with 50 women of the same colour as you, somehow you have accomplished everything you set out to accomplish. I don't think so. Not at all, why are you meeting?

Almost every year black students at Stonybrook where I teach, come around to say to me that they want to hold a meeting and I say yes, and I ask what's it about. They say unity and I say unity for what? I am already black and you are black so we unify okay but I don't need to meet with you about that. When we get together, what's the purpose of that, what do you want to do? I don't need to sit in a room with other people who are black to know that I am black – that's not unity. Unity has to have some purpose to it otherwise we are not talking politics. I don't know what we are talking, maybe a mode of social life. That's okay, but beyond that people have to begin to understand that just because somebody is a woman or

111

somebody is black does not mean that he or she and I should have the same politics. I don't think that's necessarily the case.

We should try to measure each other on the basis of what we do for each other rather than on the basis of who we are.

Pratibha: There has been a strong tendency in the women's movement to create hierarchies of oppression. What is your experience of this?

June: I have a tremendous instinctive aversion to the idea of ranking oppression. In other words for nobody to try and corner misery. I think it's dangerous. It seems to me to be an immoral way of going about things. The difficulty here is the sloppiness of language. We call everything an oppression, going to the dentist is an oppression, then the word does not mean anything. Revisions in our language might help and it might also steer us clear from saying something as useless as, but mine is this and yours is that. If I, a black woman poet and writer, a professor of English at State University, if I am oppressed then we need another word to describe a woman in a refugee camp in Palestine or the mother of six in a rural village in Nicaragua or any counterpart inside South Africa.

Pratibha: In the last few years there has been much talk about the need for coalitions and alliances between different groups of women not only nationally but internationally. What is your assessment of this form of political organising?

June: I would say about coalitions what I said about unity, which is what for? The issue should determine the social configuration of politics. I am not going to sit in a room with other people just to demonstrate black unity, we have got to have some reason for unity. Why should I coalesce with you and why do you coalesce with me? There has to be a reason why we need each other. It seems to me that an awareness of the necessity for international coalition should not be hard to come by in many spheres of feminist discourse because so many of our problems, apparently have universal currency. I think that never having been to London, for example, I can still be quite sure that most women here, whatever class or colour, are going to feel shy about walking out at night just as I do. I just assume that. That's about safety in the street. There is a universal experience for women, which is that physical mobility is circumscribed by our gender and by the enemies of our gender. This is one of the ways they seek to make us know their hatred and respect it. This holds throughout the world for women and literally we are not to move about in the world freely. If we do then we have to understand that we may have to pay for it with our bodies. That is the threat. They don't ask you what you are doing in the street, they rape you and mutilate you bodily to let you remember your place. You have no rightful place in public.

Everywhere in the world we have the least amount of income, everywhere in the world the intensity of the bond between women is seen to be subversive and it seems to me there would be good reasons to attempt international work against some of these common conditions. We cannot eliminate the problems unless we see them in their global dimensions. We should not fear the enlargement of our deliberate connections in this way. We should understand that this is a source of strength. It also makes it more difficult for anyone to destroy our movement. Okay, they can do whatever they want to in London, but there is Bangladesh, it's hydra-headed, it's happening everywhere, you can't destroy it. That's not to negate the necessity or obviate the need to work where you live but this is only part of a greater environment. I am talking against short-sightedness.

I also think it's a good idea not to have any fixed notions in one's head. I don't want any one to tell me where I should put my attention first. If down the line we can try to respect each other according to the principle of self-determination then we can begin to move forward. There are enough of us to go around and you don't have to do what I do and vice versa. I do this and you do that, there is plenty of room.

Notes

[1] Val Amos, Gail Lewis, Amina Mama and Pratibha Parmar (eds), 'Many Voices, One Chant: Black Feminist Perspectives' in *Feminist Review*, Routledge 1984, No.17, p2.

Identity

[2] *Ibid.*, pp84-9.

[3] Lynne Segal, *Is the Future Female? Troubled Thoughts on Contemporary Feminism*, Virago Press, London 1987, pp56-61.

[4] Hazel Carby, 'White Women Listen! Black Feminism and the Boundaries of Sisterhood', in Centre for Contemporary Cultural Studies (ed.), *The Empire Strikes Back: Race and Racism in 70s*, Hutchinson, London 1982, pp212-35.

[5] Gail Lewis and Pratibha Parmar, 'Black Feminism: Shared Oppression, New Expression', in *City Limits*, 4-10 March 1983.

[6] Val Amos *et al.*, *op.cit.*

[7] S. Grewal, J. Kay, L. Lander, G. Lewis and P. Parmar, *Charting the Journey: Writings by Black and Third World Women*, Sheba, London 1988.

[8] Michèle Barrett and Mary McIntosh, 'Ethnocentrism and Socialist-Feminist Theory', in *Feminist Review*, Routledge 1985, No.23.

[9] See Ramazongolu, Kazi, Lees and Mirza, 'Feedback: Feminism and Racism', in *Feminist Review*, Routledge 1986, No.22; and Kum-Kum Bhavnani and Margaret Coulson, 'Transforming Socialist-Feminism: the Challenge of Racism', in *Feminist Review*, Routledge 1986, No.23.

[10] S.Grewal *et al.*, *op.cit.*, p3.

[11] Lynne Segal, *op.cit.*, p243.

[12] Stuart Hall, 'Minimal Selves', in *ICA Documents*, London 1987, No.6, p45.

[13] June Jordan was born in Harlem and raised in Brooklyn. She is the author of several award-winning books which include six volumes of poetry and two collections of political essays. Her poems and reviews have appeared in *The New York Times, The Nation, Essence* magazine and elsewhere. Two collections of her work, *Lyrical Campaigns: Selected Poems* and *Moving Towards Home: Selected Essays* have been published in 1989 by Virago.

[14] Pratibha Parmar, 'Other Kinds of Dreams: an Interview with June Jordan', in *Spare Rib*, October 1987.

STRATEGIES OF REPRESENTATION

Photography and the politics of representation inevitably raise questions of race, gender and sexuality. Such discussions are inextricably linked to critical debates and analysis within black cultural politics in Britain as well as to the initial explorations for frameworks and parameters to discuss the nature of, and/or necessity for, critical black aesthetics.

Much of the initial oppositional practice of black photographers has been concerned with deconstructing the 'naturalness' of power relations in dominant photographic representations which position black people in an unequal relationship to white society. The struggle to deconstruct dominant imagery of black people is and has been a central one for most black photographers. Such a practice of subverting photographic orthodoxies, challenging the 'naturalness' of photographic norms and thereby undermining the assumptions and ideologies of dominant discourses, is crucial. This critical role extends to exposing the ways in which photographic institutions perpetuate and encourage the production and reproduction of images that do not contradict the dominant interests of society. These ideological strangleholds have been slowly eroded through the various interventions that black photographers have initiated in recent years, which have begun to transform the ideological basis of dominant white photographic discourses. The postmodernist tactic of their interventions lays emphasis on 'difference', on 'otherness' and 'plurality', and rejects the hegemonic drive towards universality which in the past has effectively served to suppress 'minority' voices and perspectives.

Controlling the production of images of ourselves and our communities is a stridently self-conscious strategy for many black photographers. Historically, photographic images of black people all over the world have been captured by intrepid white photographers looking for the 'exotic', the 'different', the 'anthropological native types' for 'local colour' – creating myths, fictions and fantasies which have in turn shaped the nature of encounters between contemporary black and migrant settlers and the predominantly white populace of the metropolis.

Systems of representation have spawned ideological constructs which reduce black and migrant people to a distorted and humiliated humanity – often reflecting the dominant culture's fears and anxieties about 'alien' presence and supposed threat. Cultures of domination in the metropolis have consistently defined black people as the pathological 'Other'. Differences of skin colour have become the signifiers of diminished humanity and intellectual and cultural inferiority; black people are represented as savages and natives who have not yet progressed into adulthood and therefore by implication into full humanity.

Images play a crucial role in defining and controlling the political and social power to which both individuals and marginalised groups have access. The deeply ideological nature of imagery determines not only how other people think about us but how we think about ourselves. Because of this understanding, many migrant and black women photographers are concerned with both representation and self-representation – a process which also guides the formation and construction of identities around gender, race, culture, sexuality and class. It is in representing elements of the 'self', which are considered 'other' by dominant systems of representation that an act of reclamation, empowerment and self-definition occurs.

Avoiding Essentialism

Issues of identity are often exposed and reworked in the process of making photographic images. The social and psychological construction of identities is an ongoing process which defies any notion of essential or static determinants. Identities are never fixed but complex, differentiated and are constantly repositioned. For migrant and black people who have been disenfranchised and are outside the dominant modes of representation, personal identity is very often tied to the need to articulate a collective identity around race and culture even though as individuals we inhabit a range of positions within our histories and inside our diverse identities. It has to be stressed that while many photographers are concerned with similar issues around race, gender and sexuality they often approach these in different ways: This is not merely a question of strategy but much more a reflection of both the plurality of responses to these differences, and the divergent engagements with the political nature

of photography.

Oppositional photographic practices have helped many black photographers to articulate better issues about identity, yet the problem remains that there are expectations of what the content of images produced by black photographers should be. Racial and gendered identities can sometimes be both confining and limiting in the ways in which they predefine the nature of images and themes that black photographers should/can engage with, often stultifying creative explorations into uncharted territories.

The struggle over definitions of racial identities periodically rears its head across the broad spectrum of the black cultural arena. The idea of blackness which in the past has enabled different cultural and racial communities to form alliances and engage in collective political struggle seems to be foregrounded in recent times as an area for contestation. For some of us there has always been a vigilance against the ensnarement of crypto-nationalist sentiments which rely on biologistic definitions of race, yet it is once again becoming increasingly important to restate certain basic 'first principles' which have provided the *modus operandi* for many black activists in the past – race is a social and political construction and racial identities are created in and through particular historical moments. If the unifying strength of 'blackness' is diminishing because it has become an organising category purely of a nationalist discourse, responsible for wasted energies and political fragmentation, then the time is ripe for a radical reassessment. Racial identity alone cannot be a basis for collective organising since the black communities are as beset with divisions over culture, sexuality and class as any other community. Class divisions among black communities are real in the influence they have over both the consumption and production of particular cultural objects and practices.

These observations have an added pertinence since strains of nationalism appear to have wafted through some of the more sophisticated discourses of black cultural politics; indeed there is an essentialist slant not only in some of the work produced by black women photographers, but also in the very process of naming the multi-accented matrix of black women's identities. There is a need to guard against the erroneous notion that there is innate

Souvenirs and trinkets

legitimacy in the simple proclamation of an identity as a black woman photographer.

The black communities of Britain have discontinuous histories and have been culturally and socially displaced through migration, slavery, indentured labour and as political refugees and exiles. The concept of diaspora, which embraces the plurality of these different histories and cultural forms, allows access to the diversity of articulations around identity and cultural expression. It also offers a way out of the essentialism of certain notions of blackness which refuse to acknowledge or understand the transitory nature of historical and political moments.

Stuart Hall has been much quoted on his assertion about black cultural production that:

> we have come out of the age of innocence ... which says that it's good if it's there. Provided some image of black people which they can recognise is available, it's all right. The next phase is when we actually begin to recognise the extraordinary complexity of ethnic difference and cultural difference.[2]

The question arises as to how a 'coming to knowledge' can be, or indeed is, acted upon. It seems to me that such a recognition may be leading some cultural producers and commentators into a cul-de-sac of ethnic exclusivity. There is a worrying trend in the black arts and cultural arena of selective representations in publications, exhibitions and cultural events of particular migrant and black communities. This practice is both detrimental in itself and in contradiction to the overall trajectory which argues *against* the 'structured' absence of race within wider cultural debates. There is a need for specificity in talking about race, but also a corresponding need for vigilance against such ethnic exclusivity – otherwise there is a very real danger (which we are already witnessing) of groups carving out their ethnic territories and laying claim to their individual fragments. This constitutes a trend which cannot be ignored in discussions around race, representation and black cultural politics.

This problem is too often exacerbated by the exigencies imposed by funding bodies and at the institutionalised racism prevalent in grant-giving organisations. At the heart of the political

or cultural codings.

economy of funding for black arts is the idea of ethnic absolutism: unless particular groups fit into the fixed definitions of 'black' and 'ethnic' access to funds and resources is limited.

Finding a Visual 'Voice'

Apart from a few token representations, the majority of migrant and black women photographers remain on the periphery of both alternative and mainstream photographic discourses. The opportunities for migrant and black women photographers to produce their images, get them distributed and/or exhibited are extremely meagre. Very few of these photographers are able to earn their living as professional photographers. It almost goes without saying that the reasons for this are all to do with racial, economic, cultural and sexual marginalisation and nothing to do with expertise or skill. Some women feel that such marginalisation has occurred within the predominantly male black photographic networks as much as the white feminist agencies.

The thematic concerns in the work of the diverse groups of migrant and black women photographers are as varied as the women themselves. Some of these women have gained a modicum of public profile in the last five years primarily through self-organisational activity such as the mounting of exhibitions and the publication of catalogues and journals.

Reflecting our political and personal realities, making our cultures, our experiences and ourselves visible, filling in the absences, challenging the stereotypes, disrupting assumptions and centring the black subject are guiding strategies for many migrant and black women photographers. While the common experiences of migration, cultural dislocation and racism are prevalent in the work of some of these women, it is the complexity of these experiences rather than the homogeneity that emerges.

The motivating factors behind many of the women's photographic projects are numerous yet there are certain dominant themes. The need to *document* and *record* the lives of black people, in particular black women, features strongly. The recording of history as it is lived in the 'here and now', from a non-dominant perspective, represents a refusal of historical marginality, as Brenda Agard says:

Identity

It is important that we have records of how it was and how it is. It is important that we have a record that does not distort the truths ... That when our children check our story books they have access to a detailed account of how it was for us: not just the perpetuated lies that are formed by other media ...'[3]

There is also the need to assert the 'right to create' as black women photographers. As Mumtaz Karimjee so eloquently puts it:

Tired
of struggling
for my right
to create.
Tired of struggling
with the politics and
ethnics
surrounding my right
to photograph
I retreat
to create.[4]

In the face of invisibility, marginalisation and tokenism many migrant and black women have created spaces for the production and exhibition of their work. For example, the publication in 1987 of *Polareyes*: a journal by and about black women working in photography, was the first magazine of its kind attempting to 'include the many voices of black women who have been silenced by their absence from mainstream and alternative photography magazines be they white male or white female dominated'.[5]

While there has been only one publication devoted to developing a discourse around black women and photography there have been several exhibitions. Aurat Shakti was an exhibition involving collaboration by community workers with photographers on images of Asian women whose purpose was 'to create "nana chaubi" (different pictures) and ... to do that in a way that is determined by and controlled by ourselves'.[6]

Another example, titled 'Our Space in Britain' (an exhibition by Migrant/Immigrant and Black women at Camerawork) came out of workshops organised by Maria Luiza de Melo Carvalho. Her aim was to 'create a space for migrant/immigrant/black women to work together in photography ... towards an end product which will include images which can reflect our cultures, as a result of our self-expression'.[7] The exhibition itself consists of the work of nine women from the workshop, farming a rich and textured portfolio of thematically and culturally diverse concerns.

These women explore their personal histories through symbols, objects and landscapes that signify their status as migrants, finding visual links with their cultural and collective histories. The positive affirmation of a cultural and sexual identity is a strong theme in the work of Mariagrazia Pecoraro:

> As an immigrant I am always reminded to remember my foreignness and at the same time to wipe my cultural identity away in order to fit in and not to threaten the British way of life. Starting from my own experience as an immigrant and a lesbian I am trying to develop a visual and textual language that reflects my existence in this society.[8]

This need to reject classification of our subjectivities as migrant and black women into polarities is evident in the work of Mitra Tabrizian. Her triptych of images titled 'The Blues' investigates the construction of 'difference' through masculinity/femininity and white/black, focusing on ambivalence and contradictions around sexuality and racism. Her work is complex, stimulating and challenging because it refuses simply binary divisions and is concerned too with the role of desire and fantasy in the construction of identity.

> As a feminist and someone who wants to work against racism, I want to explore the idea of the non-fixation of meaning or identity ... My work is geared towards problematising the fixation of definitions.[9]

Representing Complexity

While it remains a priority for many black cultural activists to deconstruct and decode, there is also a movement towards reconstructing and recoding. This is by no means a linear journey or a matter of 'stages of development' but should be seen as a component of a wider matrix which articulates a multiplicity of concerns over representation. It is equally crucial that, in the rush to harmonise our differences, the specificities of response that black photographers have made to our contradictory realities are not obscured. The fact that differences exist has to be acknowledged and any common ground has to be actively created and negotiated.

There is evidence that a more critical engagement with photographic imagery and practices is underway. But we need to discern between those photographic projects and images concerned with notions of contesting racist stereotypes of black people – their subject matter being dependent on and defined by dominant representations, and those photographic images which, while concerned with the politics of racism, are equally keen to interrogate the politics of representation itself. The latter strategy allows greater creative diversity because it is free from the constraints and pressures of substituting 'positive images' for 'negative images', moving us away from simplistic notions of stereotypes. Finally it is important that the development of an organic engagement with the political nature of imagery and photographic practices continues to take place both within black photography in general and migrant and black women's photography specifically.

Notes

[1] *Ten:8*, 'Black Experiences', Issue 22, p30. This includes a resource list of major initiatives taken by black photographers, many of which culminated in 'Autograph' – the Association of Black Photographers (Unit 135, One Marche Building, 444 Brixton Road, London SW9).
[2] Stuart Hall, 'New Ethnicities' in *Black Film British Cinema*, ICA Document No.7, London.
[3] *Polareyes*, distributed by Turnaround Distribution, London.
[4] *Ibid.*, p27.
[5] *Ibid.*, p3.
[6] 'Aurat Shakti' is available for hire from the Cockpit Gallery, Princeton Street, London WC1.
[7] 'Our Space in Britain', from the exhibition catalogue. 'Our Space in Britain' is available for hire from Camerawork, 121 Roman Road, London E2.
[8] *Ten:8*, 'Body Politic' Issue 25.
[9] *Ibid.*

I would like to thank Shaheen Haque, Mumtaz Karimjee, Claudette Williams, Shaila Shah, Sona Osman, Vron Ware, Paul Gilroy and Isaac Julien for their support, friendship and hours of useful discussions and Usha Brown for her timely encouragement. My special thanks to June Jordan for her friendship and inspiration.

Live for Sharam and die for Izzat

ZARINA BHIMJI

SHE SPLITS THE PERSONALITY IN TWO:

Each night his advances become more demanding –

She tells herself she will run away before she is forced to . . . .

He would come beside her pillow every night. She turned into her OTHERSELF.

For many years she did not remember much.

BLOOD SPREADS OUT,

THERE WILL NOT BE DARKNESS OR BRIGHTNESS IN ANY DIRECTION.

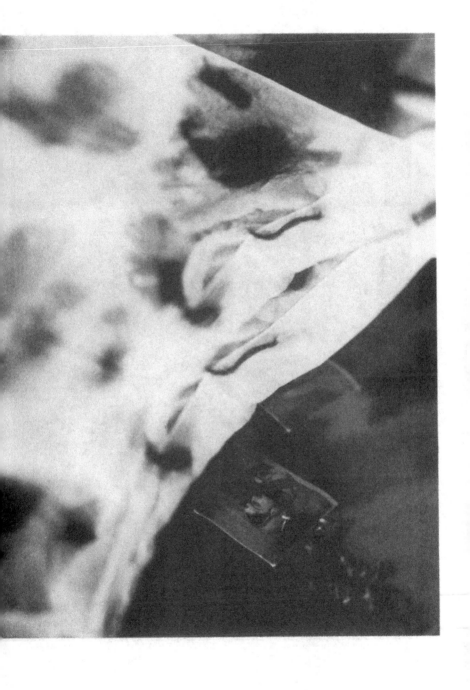

HER OTHERSELF BLURTS INTO HYSTERICAL WEEPING:

She has been left to rationalise the truth –

Rage pours out.

From her nipples pus pours, as if from a sieve.

When she wakes up she is in a puddle of pus. With distaste she cleans herself up.

Rage pours out, devastating everything in its path.

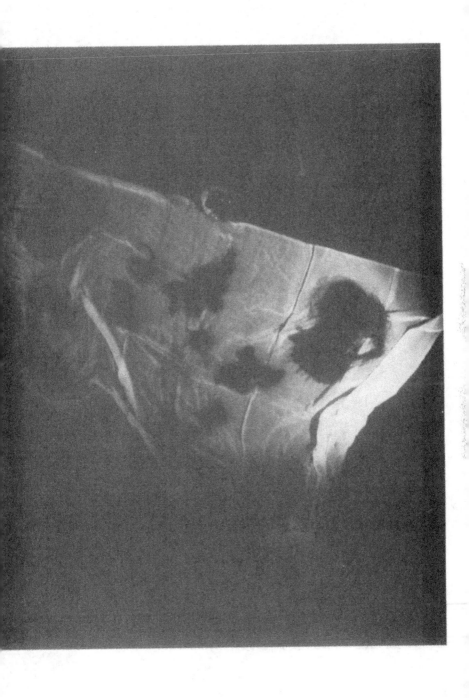

TODAY MY HEART IS IN ANXIETY:

Girlfriends paint her hands with henna and rub her body with jasmin oil,

Preparing her for the . . .

on her pale hand the henna's delicate stain – reminds her of how they have

changed . . . SHE WRITES:

Dear Bapa, there are so many things i hate of you,

Mostly, what i hate is your flesh, i hate it because . . . because . . . she

Sobs and Sobs, the sound is terrible to hear, she feels sick as well as

bitter, after taste of guilt, Guilt for father hate.

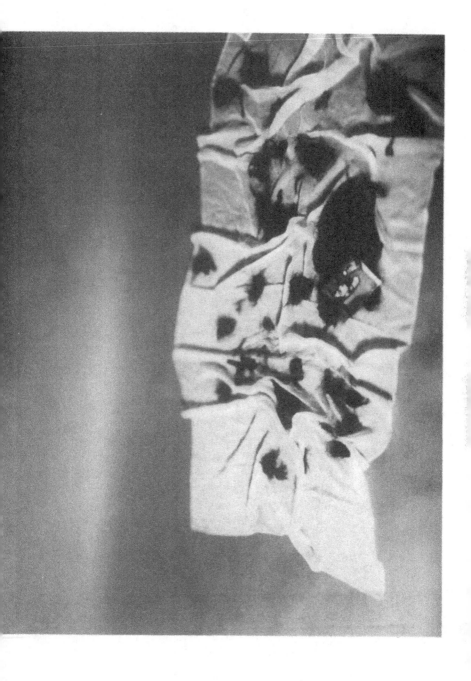

FEELS HERSELF PASSING IN AND OUT OF CONSCIOUSNESS:

I feel nausea, my headache comes back, I think I'm going to be sick.

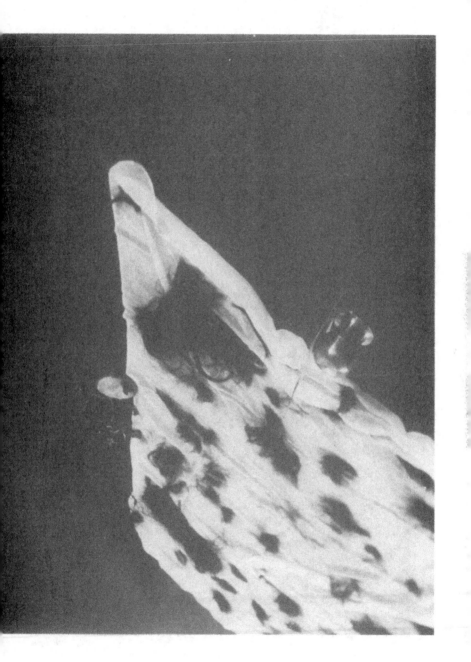

Time is slipping, SHE is overcome with sudden loneliness, she sees his body stiff. FEELING as if a bomb were tick tick ticking in her chest, SHE is resentful. "You don't own me or owe to me."

NOBODY DOES . . . .

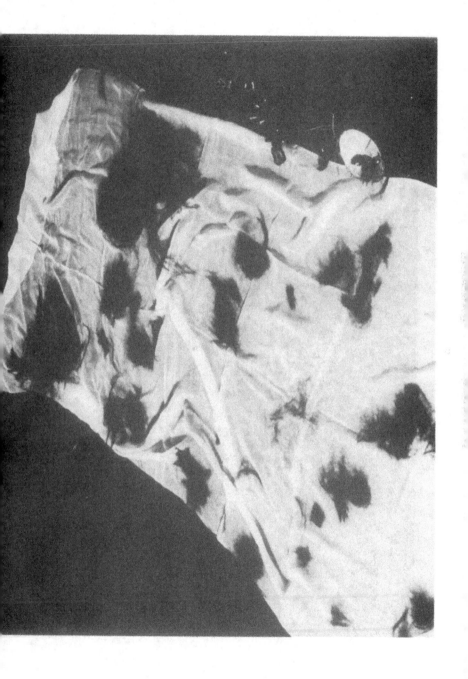

HER LIFE IS WRECKED, KISMET.

"Why do you fall at your Father's feet and touch your forehead to

the ground?"

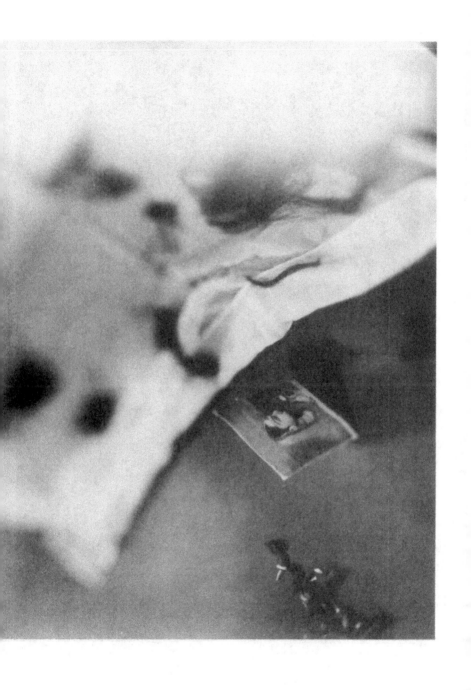

Anyway, what YOU do in Britain, does it really count?

Aunt Nilofar's voice cracked with anger: "What kind of a man is he?"

He . . . has NO IZZAT . . .

Once Aurat loses Izzat, She has no support, it's a high price to pay . . .

She lay on her bed, shrivelled lip moving in constant prayer,

THE SMELL IS CREEPING INTO HER SILENCE

The Sari is given up for jeans, yet, the colour of one's skin, and eyes still

remains . . . it does not leave . . .

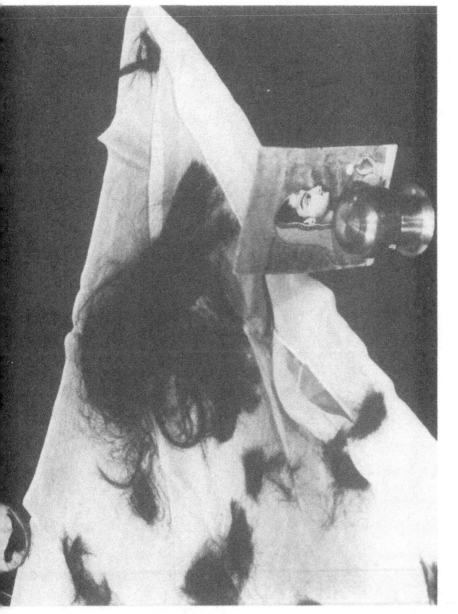

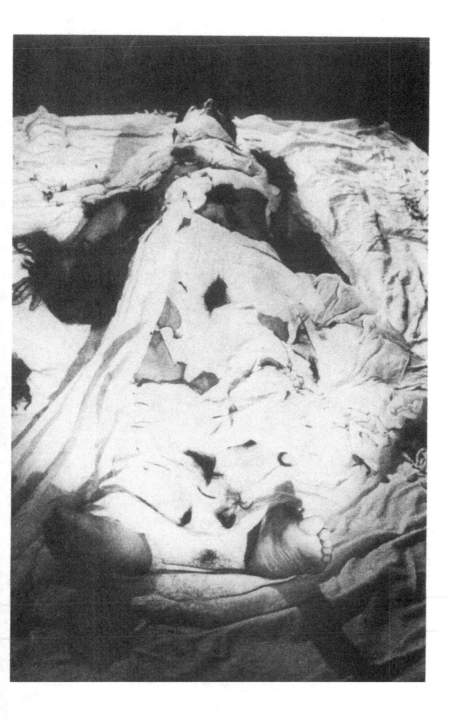

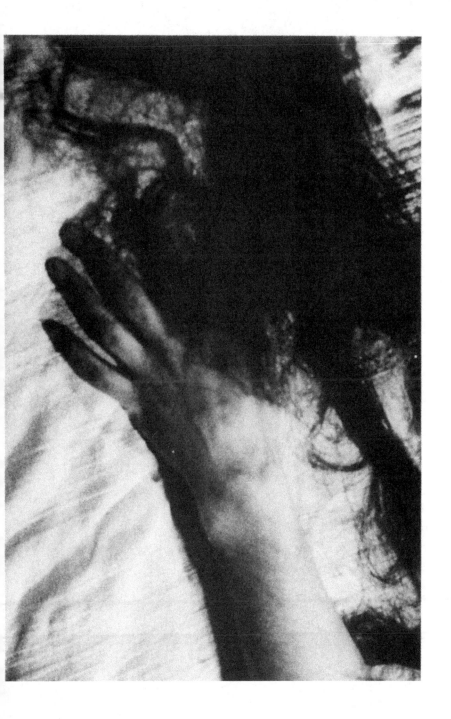

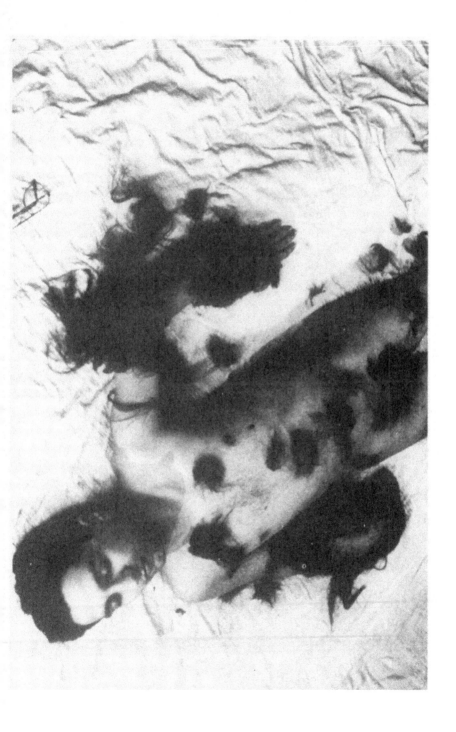

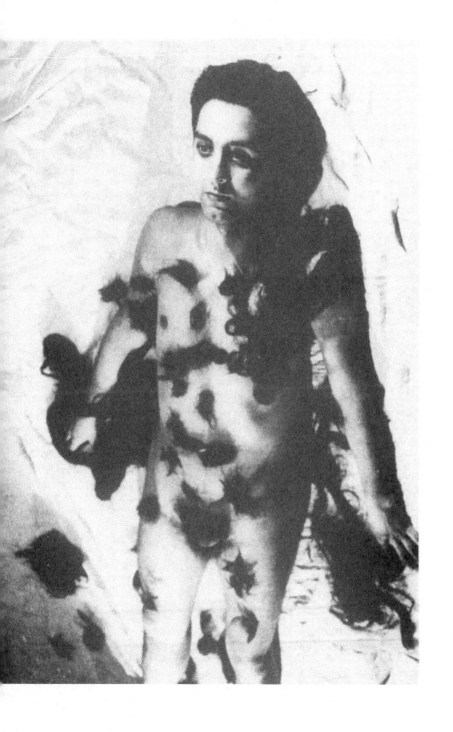

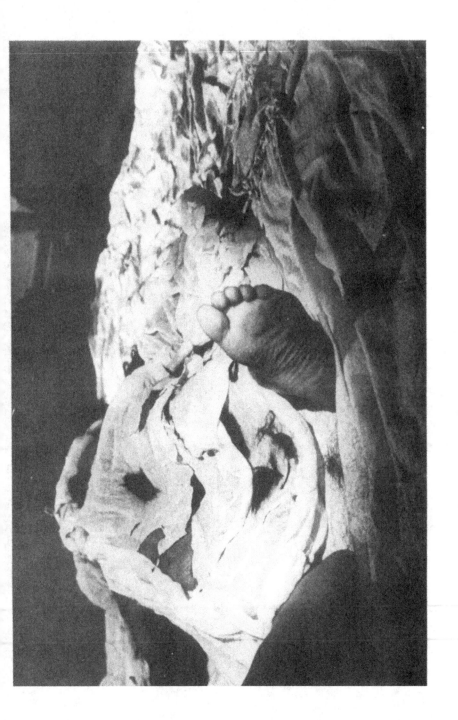

Notes

This series of photographs were originally commissioned by the Photographers' Gallery, London, for the exhibition 'Intimate Distance' (1989). In that exhibition they were displayed as an installation, printed on lith film and suspended from the ceiling, giving the appearance of large, dimly lit glass slides. The exhibition is available from the Photographers' Gallery.

Special thanks to Kanwaljit Sangha.

Practices of Freedom: 'Citizenship' and the Politics of Identity in the Age of AIDS

SIMON WATNEY

The tradition of the oppressed teaches us that the 'state of emergency' in which we live is not the exception but the rule ... The current amazement that the things we are experiencing are 'still' possible in the twentieth century is *not* philosophical. This amazement is not the beginning of knowledge – unless it is the knowledge that the view of history that gives rise to it is untenable.

Walter Benjamin, *Theses on the Philosophy of History*, No.8 (1940)

A legally unrestricted majority rule, that is, a democracy without a constitution, can be very formidable in the suppression of the rights of minorities and very effective in the suffocation of dissent without any use of violence. But that does not mean that violence and power are the same.

Hannah Arendt, *On Violence* (1970)

The relentlessly deepening AIDS crisis raises profound questions for all nations, ranging from community needs to adequate health-care provision. This is especially the case in the United Kingdom, where the epidemic coincides with a major ideological dispute about medical and welfare entitlements, and a sustained government critique of socialised medicine, in theory and in practice. Conflict in health and welfare policy reflects a wider debate that increasingly addresses the entire structure of British

157

parliamentary politics, as an increasingly pluralistic model of European politics is met with strong government resistance in the name of national sovereignty.

The publication of Charter 88 has been widely taken to represent a major sea change in British politics. The Charter drew attention to the erosion of civil rights in the UK, claiming that 'a traditional British belief in the benign nature of the country's institutions encourages an unsystematic perception of these grave matters'.[1] It argued that 'the intensification of authoritarian rule has only recently begun', though it is worth pointing out that the emergence of the 'new social movements' since 1968 has been firmly grounded in a critique of parliamentarianism. It is also important to draw attention to that central strand of British socialism, from Thomas Paine to Raymond Williams, which has sustained a profound and complex critique of the meaning and practice of democracy as it has been instituted in Britain. From both these perspectives it is clear that the increasingly *confident* authoritarianism of British government in the 1980s has only been possible because of the archaic nature of Britain's political institutions and political culture. Whilst this repressive current has seemingly only recently come to the attention of the mainstream of British politics, it has long been apparent to those whom parliamentary democracy has never recognised as legitimate political subjects or constituencies.

In this essay I want to consider the question of civil liberties in relation to the heavily contested concept of citizenship. As Stuart Hall and David Held have pointed out:

> Like all the key contested political concepts of our time, it can be appropriated within very different political discourses and articulated to very different political positions – as its recuperation by the New Right clearly shows.[2]

Rather than attempt a historical survey of the concept of citizenship in British political theory and practice, I want to consider its potential for forging identities and alliances that are independent of traditional forms of party and government allegiance. I also want to consider citizenship in relation to a particular site of controversial political activity: that of lesbian and gay responses to the AIDS crisis. This raises profound ethical and constitutional issues that the

Left has not begun to consider: as the American critic Douglas Crimp points out, the AIDS epidemic is not simply a natural disaster, but on the contrary, it has been *allowed to happen*.[3] The emergence in 1989 of two new national lesbian and gay civil rights organisations in Britain suggest the emergence of a new politics of sexuality which is sensitive to recent debates concerning the construction of subjectivity, and able to reach out beyond older notions of the rights of supposedly distinct 'sexual minorities'.[4] This returns us to the urgent question of the role of ethics in the construction of political identities that might offer a coherent collective refusal of both the values of capitalism and the institutions of parliamentarianism as it is currently practised and understood.

Subjects or Citizens?

In *Towards 2000* Raymond Williams offered what is perhaps the most coherent modern socialist critique of British parliamentary democracy. For Williams this was not merely 'some abstract or theoretical argument', as he pointed out:

> The British Parliament, strictly speaking, is not an institution but an assembly of three bodies, of which only one is elected. ... The House of Lords, controlled by heredity rather than by election, is often seen as residual: a contradiction of the ideology of electoral democracy. It is indeed a contradiction of the ideology, in terms of the actual constitution it may not be the House of Lords but the House of Commons that is anomalous. For the sovereignty of the British State is not in the British People, as in most electoral democracies, but in this special definition of the 'Crown in Parliament'. British adults are not citizens, but legally, *subjects*, in that old term derived from absolute monarchy.[5]

From a very different political perspective, Michael Elliott notes that if a British government

> wants to restrict the liberty of its subjects, it may do so by seeking parliamentary approval for legislation in a manner identical to the approval it would seek for the power to build a new lighthouse. Once passed, decisions taken under the civil liberty-restraining legislation are different in legal kind not a whit from those taken in any other,

mundane, concern of government. They are subject to no special procedures, susceptible to no special reviews.[6]

British governments are thus empowered to stamp on any aspect of civil society with complete impunity, and as Elliott points out, although the Labour Party has consistently attacked the Tory record of attacks on civil liberties,

> it has not less consistently refused to commit itself to anything like a Bill of Rights designed to guarantee civil liberties. Instead, it takes the view that the constraints in any such Bill would be more trouble than they are worth.[7]

It remains a cruel irony of British political life that civil rights are widely interpreted as if they were the property of the Right, by the Right, and of the Left, by the Left. Both sides of the party political divide have worked tirelessly to deny rights to those whom they perceive as their adversaries, or whom they have been unable to recognise as *having* rights in the first place. Thus the fields of race relations, trade unionism and sexual politics, have been especially contested areas, where individual groups have frequently had to lobby *outside* the party political system as a whole in order to establish their needs. This has given rise to a large number of situations in which basically incompatible estimations of civil rights are disputed. These raise profound questions concerning the validity of the wider legitimating ideology of British democratic 'freedom', which is under severe stress from several sources such as the increasingly political role of the police as a direct agency of governments, the role of the judiciary in labour disputes, the relations between the media and the state, and a relentless increase in legal moralism, of which Section 28 of the 1988 Local Government Bill was but one clear example.[8]

As has been widely noted, Thatcherism has employed a persuasive anti-statist rhetoric to buttress its definiton of individual rights, which are reduced to the level of consumption in the market-place. Labourism meanwhile has been trapped between its traditional commitment to notions of class struggle as the primary site of political activity and its own version of consumer individualism. The Left has thus been largely unable to respond to areas of political and ideological contestation that have not seemed to back directly onto the jousting ground of Westminster, for electoral advantage is always *the* central issue in a first-past-the-post electoral system. Moreover, the Labour Party has since its inception 'bought into' parliamentarianism in a largely uncritical manner. This 'investment' inevitably serves to increase cynicism in the electorate, and has led to the unfortunate situation of the 1980s in which calls for major constitutional reform, that possess a tremendous potential for enlarging the popular estimation and practice of democracy, are dismissed as 'marginal' by most leading figures in the Conservative and Labour parties alike. The Labour Party's grudging, belated acknowledgement of feminism and environmentalism has evidently derived less from questions of ethical principle than current tactical calculations, defined within the narrow terms of established parliamentary electoral politics. Yet sooner rather than later, an overall political system which privileges either class factors or 'free'-market forces to the virtual exclusion of other issues will prove to be *culturally* redundant.[9]

For it is precisely the broad spectrum of issues raised by environmentalist, anti-racist, health-related and sexual politics *outside* the major parties that already constitutes the clearest site of a collective anti-Thatcherite agenda, even if its various emphases and elements have no *necessary* connection. It is the special tragedy of the 1980s that there is no obvious political party that can even imagine the task of aligning or uniting these disparate sites of struggle. This has particular implications for the concept of citizenship, which in theory at least offers a strong potential for a reintegration of the individual in socialist politics as something rather more than a mere agent of inexorable economic and hisotrical forces. Citizenship offers a concrete, practical alternative to Marx's celebrated critique of bourgeois individualism, with its familiar postulation of the 'abstract – isolated – human individual' as the imagined source of all human activity, prior to and independent of all social relations.[10] For on the one hand it can admit the emergence of a politics which embraces but also exceeds questions of wage-labour, whilst on the other it provides a secure ground for the establishment of *collective* rights, for which Anglo-American society shows scant regard.[11] As Raymond Williams argued in the early 1980s, the present political system directs us only towards party politics at all effective levels:

> It is equally clear that the central function of these parties is to reproduce the existing definitions of issues and interests. When they extend to new issues or interests, they usually lead back into a system which will isolate, dilute and eventually compromise them. If there is one thing that should have been learned in the years since 1945, it is this … In their present forms the parties are practically constituted to be like this. They absorb and deflect new issues and interests in their more fundamental process of reproducing and maximising their share of the existing and governing dispositions.[12]

As I have pointed out elsewhere, for well over a century, parliamentarianism has attempted to stifle

> the emergence of the types of popular politics rooted in notions of constitutional rights, which are so deeply constitutive of the political institutions and cultural identities of other European nations. British politics have rarely attempted to acknowledge the difficulties of addressing different population groups in Britain from a pluralist perspective. This is reflected in the strong resistance to constitutional reform, and the ways in which our archaic and profoundly undemocratic voting system, together with the bizarre assemblage of the House of Commons, the non-elected House of Lords, and the monarchy, are widely regarded as evidence of some imagined national superiority, rather than as sadly accurate indicators of our national political backwardness and chauvinism.[13]

It has only been at the level of *local* government, that the British Left has been able to learn from such obvious European examples of a politics of cultural diversity as the Italian Communist Party's (PCI) regular L'Unità festivals that take place throughout Italy, bringing together farmers and film-makers, feminists and Fiat workers – as, for example, in the Glasgow People's Palace project, and the wider cultural politics of the Greater London Council, with its serious commitment to the needs of its many social constituencies. It was precisely because of its commitment to a model of democratic pluralism that the GLC was abolished by the Conservative government, without any democratic consultation with the population of greater London. Thus the overall structure of British party politics has only been able to respond to the emergence of 'identity politics' by reducing them to the status of single issues, to be appended faithfully to manifestos, and consigned to conference resolutions where they can languish in worthy oblivion. Any threat that they might pose to the authority of parliamentarianism as such is safely deflected back into the traditional terms of parliament itself. The overnight 'greening' of party political rhetoric after the sweeping success of the Greens in the 1989 European parliamentary elections is only the most glaringly obvious example of this general phenomenon. So we may fairly detect a growing gulf between the actual aspirations of large sections of the population of the UK, and their petrified reflection in the electoral calculations that dictate the political institutions which claim to represent them. This guarantees an ever-increasing cynicism concerning the very concept of politics, and a profoundly painful ambivalence on the part of those who find their particular areas of political acitivity hijacked by forces that would in all other circumstances evidently prefer to ignore them altogether. This is extremely unhealthy in a country which is best described as pre-democratic, at least in comparison to most of our European Community (EC) partners.

We thus face an extremely difficult and paradoxical situation in terms of developing immediate strategies over and above the simple wish to dislodge Thatcherism. As David Marquand has argued:

> As long as the Labour Party thinks of absolutist power it will not embrace electoral reform, and as long as it refuses to embrace electoral reform it will be hopelessly divided from pluralist politics ... The leadership is stuck in the Bourbon thinking of the early 1950s, which says: 'If you have a Bill of Rights you give power to unelected judges [and that] means the elected parliament loses power. That is intolerable because we stand for the elected parliament having total power'. That is a completely ... different view of politics and citizenship and the rights of the citizen in society.[14]

The baronial ambitions of the Labour leadership were lamentably obvious at the 1989 Party conference, when modest calls for no more than the establishment of a working party on electoral reform were overwhelmingly rejected, after the party's deputy leader argued that this would be 'an act of historic folly', on the curious grounds that:

> It is in the House of Commons that governments build there majorities.
> For the House of Commons, proportional representation would in
> consequence be a reduction, not an extension of democracy.[15]

It was sadly apparent that the Labour Party is ill-prepared to
consider seriously taking up the larger ethical questions concerning
the *principles* of political representation, in spite of arguments by
Jeff Rooker MP and others that the present electoral system
guarantees a parliamentary politics that is 'largely middle-class,
white and male-dominated' and he added that:

> Electoral reform cannot be held in reserve in case things go wrong. It
> would be unprincipled and undemocratic to take that view.[16]

Unfortunately that is precisely the context in which questions of
electoral, and wider constitutional, reform tend to arise, as if
Thatcherism were somehow responsible for the fact of an 'elective
dictatorship' on the basis of a mere 42 per cent of the overall vote at
the 1987 general election. As Sheila Cunningham MP pointed out in
the Labour Party conference debate:

> Both the Tories and Labour had 46 per cent of the vote in the 1955
> general election, yet the Conservatives were elected with a majority of
> 55.

This reluctance or inability to consider wider aspects of the theory
and practice of British democracy leaves the Labour Party almost
entirely unable to challenge, let alone attempt to redefine, such
basic ideological building blocks in British political discourse as
notions of 'law and order', 'the national interest', or 'family values',
that have so frequently been employed as persuasive justifications
for the further curtailment of civil rights. Indeed, the Labour Party
leadership usually seems largely in sympathy with such broad,
abstract ideological formulations which provide the everyday
support for authoritarian government and the political system that
sustains it. The formal and informal conventions of British

parliamentarianism make this more or less inevitable, in such a way that we end up with the extraordinary conclusion from Roy Hattersley and others that political coalitions are *intrinsically* undesirable. No matter what the cost, a 'virile' two-party system based on absolute majorities must be preserved. This only serves further to legitimate the specifically British belief that politicians should be able to enjoy a virtually limitless exercise of power. The only exception to this golden rule seems to concern matters of sexual conduct on the part of politicians, such that politicians in the 1980s have been expected to observe 'moral standards' that would have disqualified most of the leading figures in British politics in the past hundred years and more. The surprise irony of this absurd situation is that, within certain limits, it has been Mrs Thatcher herself who has refused to surrender those whom she regards as effective politicians – such as Cecil Parkinson – to the consequences of just the type of moralistic witch-hunting that her own version of Victorian values encourage.

The same exaggerated worship of parliamentary protocols also permits the Left either to berate or to turn a Nelson-like blind eye to the economic and political limitations on British parliamentary sovereignty that *already* stem from our longstanding treaty obligations to the European Community. This leaves the Labour Party with a regrettable inability to challenge effectively the Prime Minister's controversial attitude to the wider project of European federalism – the 'Delors plan' – which is no more palatable to the narrow nationalistic thinking that determines so much of Labour's policy than it is to most Conservatives. This in turn explains at least something of Labour's traditional lack of interest in developing genuine theoretical debate within the party, and its hostility even to sympathetic contemporary socialist theorists and historians (with the exception of those who can be relied upon to denounce constitutional reform). Labour's crippling anti-intellectualism has long deafened it to many of its most able potential allies and strategists, such as the late Raymond Williams whose three minimum proposals for Britain finally to become a modern European democracy evidently failed to impress either the party leadership or the 'labour aristocracy'. Williams's agenda consists of:

Transfer of legal sovereignty to the people or their elected government; abolition of the second chamber now based on heredity and patronage, and its replacement by a differently constituted body, based on election; adoption of an electoral system which would determine the composition of an elected parliament in terms of the actual distribution of votes.[17]

None the less, it should not be assumed that the restoration of local government, the reform of the legal system, electoral reform or other democratising measures, would *of themselves* by sufficient to transform parliamentary *subjects* into self-conscious *citizens*, fully aware of their rights and obligations in a democratic society. It is therefore at least as important to develop the cultural and ideological dimensions of the concept of entitlement, in the sense that entitlements should be regarded as 'rights which are intended to be removed from the caprices of day-to-day politics'.[18] As Ralf Dahrendorf has noted, the concept of citizenship is inseparable from that of entitlement, pointing out that this involves a fundamental critique of the postwar discourse of 'welfare' whose

patronising connotations detract from the fact that it is about entitlements. Pensions and medical care, insurance against accidents, but also education and perhaps a minimum wage are civil-rights, not charitable gifts.[19]

Such an approach has the great virtue of potentially acknowledging the transformation of political subjectivities in the past thirty years, and it recognises that entitlements must be sufficiently flexible to be able to respond to the emergence of *new* social identities and constituencies. Citizenship thus stands to unite the overlapping interests of individuals and groups whose self-conscious identities are specific to the postwar period, whether in relation to race, gender, sexuality, disability, or whatever. The concept of citizenship is sensitive to the fact that our identities are multiple and mobile, that we all increasingly identify ourselves with aspects of race, class, sexuality, and so on, in ways that are idiosyncratic and subject to frequent change over time. Social identitities are not fixed in the once-and-for-all way that traditional Marxist class theory would have us believe, and as Dahrendorf suggests:

> The point about full citizenship ... is that it transforms social conflicts from all-or-nothing battles into a mechanism to bring about gradual change. As long as insuperable entitlement barriers are the issue, conflicts are a zero-sum game. One side has to give way and will lose what the other side gains ... Once citizenship rights are established, conflicts are about more or less of things which are in principle accessible to everybody.[20]

As presently constituted, British party politics has a heavy investment in just such 'zero-sum' games and has proved itself radically unable to respond to the needs of the changed and emergent social identities of recent decades. In these circumstances Thatcherism simply retreats into a fantasy of supposedly universal moral values, associated with an entirely *ideological* notion of 'the family', which seems to have considerable purchase on a period of profound social change (often felt most keenly in the domestic sphere, not least in the relations between women and men, and in patterns of child-raising). The alternatives to this very limited vision of what it might mean to be a British subject stem from an open affirmation of the changed and changing circumstances that potentially permit greater degrees of happiness and self-determination for greater numbers of people, even if these changes are derided and caricatured by Thatcherism as 'promiscuous' or 'unpatriotic'. Yet the practice of citizenship cannot be imposed from above, in the historical manner of postwar welfarism. It has to be established at the grass-roots, and institutionally located at that level, for as Raymond Williams argues:

> The only kind of socialism which now stands any chance of being established in the old industrialised bourgeois-democratic societies, is one centrally based on new kinds of communal, cooperative and collective institutions ... That is really the only road which socialists in these countries have left to travel ... The existing dominant formula of the tight party government which will deliver self-management, seems to me at best a pious hope, at worst a pathetic delusion.[21]

Identity

There is thus all the more reason that the debate about citizenship should be firmly grounded in the concrete circumstances of individual and collective social life, and in concrete questions of entitlement in contemporary Britain. The experience of lesbians and gay men in relations to AIDS in the 1980s provides just such an example. A written parliamentary answer in January 1989 revealed that no less than 35 gay men aged 16 to 21 were criminalised by the courts in Britain for consensual sexual relations above the age of consent that obtains for heterosexuals. I am not aware of a single comment on this disgraceful situation outside the gay press, which might as well be written, printed and distributed on Mars as far as the vast majority of professional commentators and politicians are concerned. Nor is the gay press's unparalleled long-term record in AIDS journalism ever acknowledged in other publications. The decision of the 1989 Labour conference to throw out the National Executive Committee's rejection of calls for a single age of consent for everyone in Britain, including gay men, strongly suggests that political debates founded upon the ethical principle of entitlements can prevail over the stubbornly entrenched prejudice and tactical electoral calculations that result in the defence of fundamentally unjust and undemocratic legal double-standards.[22]

'Family Values' and Community Needs

One of the major characteristics of Thatcherism has been the great confidence with which the government speaks and legislates in the name of 'traditional' moral values, in areas which all previous postwar administrations have regarded as highly sensitive and complex. Of these, the question of sexuality and 'the family' has been especially important: much of the government's popularity has resided in its successful presentation of 'the family' as uniquely threatened and vulnerable, and therefore in need of stringent defensive measures, mainly from lesbians and gay men who have consistently been presented as one of the gravest threats to this fantasy of uniform 'family life'. In Mrs Thatcher's personal rhetoric, 'family' and 'nation' have long been presented as mutually interchangeable terms in such a way that imagined challenges to the former can also be presented as deeply dangerous for the latter.

Again it comes as no surprise to learn that the Prime Minister was the driving force behind Clause 28 of the 1988 Local Government Bill which sought to prevent 'the promotion of homosexuality' by local authorities. The widespread acceptance of legislation against such imaginary offences, not least by the Labour front bench, is indicative of the sophistication of Thatcherism's ideological strategies, drawing on a real if regrettable legacy of anti-gay prejudice in British legal and popular culture. From the field of sex education to domestic video use, Thatcherism has sought to abolish former distinctions between the public and the private, in the name of the 'family values' that supposedly transcend all other estimations of individual and collective rights.

Yet AIDS confronts the government with a complex reality that cannot easily be disposed of in such over-simplified terms. We are not dealing with a single epidemic, but with a series of unfolding and overlapping epidemics within and between different population groups, determined by the modes of transmission of HIV in the decade or more before its existence was realised. The result has been a significant tension between conflicting imperatives. On the one hand ministers such as David Mellor congratulate organisations such as the Terrence Higgins Trust in the voluntary sector, whilst on the other, hard-line back-benchers continue to make political capital out of the crudest forms of prejudice, aided and abetted by the ever-dependable services of large sections of the British press. One consequence of this tension has been a bizarre compromise between the government's official moral ideology and the need for effective health education, which seriously suggests that recommending monogamy or celibacy is the best 'solution' to the issue of HIV infection. It is as if the actual complexity and diversity of human sexuality is as much of a problem for the government as the epidemic.

Direct censorship of health education projects produced by the government's own Health Education Authority provides shocking evidence of Thatcherism's unwavering reliance on moral homilies, which are policed at entirely unaccountable levels of executive government. An overriding commitment to a politically expedient vision of 'family values' is being sustained indefinitely, at the direct expense of effective health education strategies. This can only serve

169

to guarantee the increased transmission of HIV, especially among heterosexuals who have been comfortably cocooned in the potentially deadly delusion that they are not really at risk since the beginning of the epidemic. Given the average of ten years between HIV infection and diagnosable symptoms öf AIDS, the government's direct legacy of preventable AIDS cases will not be fully apparent until the late 1990s.

The opposition parties have all but failed to challenge the validity of the picture of British social life depicted by Thatcherite fundamentalism, or to question the government's long-term failure to acknowledge the actual complexity of the population that it claims to represent. Even political parties in opposition to Thatcherism seem uniformly unable to grasp the political dimensions of the HIV epidemic. The Left has only been able to register AIDS against the criteria of pre-existing policies and priorities. In practice, this has guaranteed an almost total silence on the entire subject. It would not be correct to conclude that the Labour NEC has simply buckled under the pressure of external anti-gay prejudice, real as this is. On the contrary, it has been fully prepared to exploit that prejudice to its own imagined electoral advantage. AIDS may be privately described as a 'disaster' or even a 'tragedy', but it is *never* publicly identified as an epidemic which in almost every respect has been, and continues to be *allowed to happen*.[23]

Since the early years of the epidemic, lesbians and gay men have been at the forefront of attempts to produce effective health education materials, for all sections of the population. Unfortunately this work has been hampered both by lack of funds, and archaic indecency and obscenity legislation. The Thatcherite model of business sponsorship for private charities has proved a disastrous failure, even for the government's own National AIDS Trust (NAT) which has failed to raise funds from the City or other commercial sources. We now face a situation in which the consequences of a decade of inadequate medical reporting in the British press has led to widespread boredom with the whole subject of AIDS, reinforced by the government's attempts to perpetrate its values on the epidemic through its own 'official' advertising campaigns, which are based on a heady brew of sexual puritanism and scare-mongering.

This is exemplified by the typically individualistic approach of the work of the Health Education Authority (HEA), whose adverts share a common by-line 'AIDS: You're as safe as you want to be'. The situation is further complicated by the fact that the HEA itself has long been under attack from the radical Right, which wishes to present AIDS as a form of direct retribution against those who wantonly fail to live lives of exclusively monogamous heterosexuality. The prevalence of this retributive view is most tragically apparent in the widespread acceptance of the belief that the success of Safer Sex campaigns amongst gay men may safely be disregarded by the rest of the population because of our 'exceptional' status. The exceptionalist argument holds that gay men constitute 'a community' which adopted Safer Sex only when we saw our friends dying around us. This is untrue and dangerously misleading, since until very recently indeed it was statistically most unlikely that most gay men had any direct experience of either HIV infection or AIDS in their immediate friendship circles. Yet Safer Sex was indeed taken up by most gay men in Britain in the mid-1980s, as official epidemiology makes perfectly plain. It is only possible to understand this refusal to learn from the demonstrably proven effectiveness of Safer Sex education amongst gay men in terms of a larger and prior inability to regard lesbians and gay men as fundamentally ordinary and intrinsically unremarkable members of British society. For that reason anti-gay prejudice continues to make heterosexuals increasingly vulnerable to HIV.

At the same time we should notice the extreme levels of prejudice and ignorance concerning the position of the thousands of gay men living with HIV or AIDS in Britain, in order to understand the full significance of the 'moral standards' that have dominated British public life in the 1980s. If there has been a dramatic resurgence of gay political activity in this period, it is hardly surprising since it has become so painfully clear that our very existence is widely regarded as regrettable. It is important to consider the full significance of the government's continuing failure to support community-based health education among the social groups most severely affected by HIV disease since 1981. We read and hear about how well 'the gay community' has done in cutting back the rate of new cases of infection, yet in reality the social relations of gay men in Britain are fragile, and the absence of a powerful model of civil rights politics has tended to undermine the emergence of a confident gay culture in Britain.

In these circumstances, community development is much the most important strategy in HIV/AIDS education, since it is based on the development and reinforcement of the sense of individual and collective worth and responsibility. HIV education among gay men has emphasised the importance of Safer Sex for all men having sex with men, regardless of their known or perceived antibody status, as opposed to official messages which continue to demonise people living with HIV.[24] A special irony of the current situation is that Section 28 has brought gay men and lesbians together as never before, in opposition to frankly anti-gay legislation, and this in itself has stimulated a strengthening of gay community values. Yet through all this, I am not aware of a single statement either from the Prime Minister or the Leader of her Majesty's Opposition that draws attention to the tragedy of an epidemic that has already affected tens of thousands throughout the UK. This resounding silence demonstrates with frightening clarity the full extent of the divorce between British parliamentary politics, and the lives of the actual subjects of Britain.

This grim separation of political priorities from the field of everyday life is still more apparent at the level of biomedical research. In the United States there are currently over 200 ongoing clinical trials of possible new treatment drugs against HIV, and the wide range of opportunistic conditions that collectively make up the Acquired Immune Deficiency Syndrome. In Britain there is only one solitary clinical trial, which largely duplicates American research. The Medical Research Council (MRC) has established a directed programme of research, which its Director has described as having 'the aim of developing vaccines for the prevention, and drugs for the treatment, of HIV infection and AIDS'.[25] Yet if one turns to the back of the MRC's guide to its *AIDS Directed Programme*, one finds committees supervising vaccine trials and the ethical aspects of vaccine research, but there is no committee supervising treatment research or the medical ethics of treatment-related clinical trials, for the simple reason that treatment research is *not* taking place. The entire bulk of more than £40 million at the MRC's disposal for HIV/AIDS research has been dedicated to the search for a vaccine for the *un*infected: people living with HIV disease have been written off in their entirety. Whilst there are excellent reasons for British scientists to wish to build on previous expertise in the field of vaccine research, it is chilling that this has been posed as an alternative to treatment research. In this context we might consider the statement by one leading MRC microbiologist that treatment research raises 'a moral dilemma', since it would 'run the risk of prolonging the lives of people who would be infectious in the community'.[26] It should be perfectly clear that the lives of people living with HIV disease, and their immediate communities are held very cheap both by official HIV education and the top levels of the MRC.

'Acting Up': the Cultural Politics of AIDS

In the United States there have been more than 100,000 diagnosed cases of AIDS since 1981, of whom more than 60,000 are already dead. The Centers for Disease Control (CDC) in Atlanta, Georgia estimate that there are at least 1.5 million people infected by HIV in the USA. Moreover, both HIV and AIDS statistics faithfully duplicate pre-existing patterns of health-care provision, economic inequalities and prejudice. For example, only 9 per cent of children with AIDS in New York are white. It was not until Thanksgiving, 1987 that the then President Reagan found himself able to utter the word 'AIDS', at a time when 25,644 people had *already* died. He announced that he had asked

> the Department of Health and Human Services to determine as soon as possible the extent to which the AIDS virus has penetrated our society.[27]

Earlier in the year a group of activists had formed the 'AIDS Coalition To Unleash Power' (ACT UP) in New York, to draw attention to the scandalous government failure to respond to the needs of the epidemic, and to put pressure on all the leading institutions managing the course of the epidemic – from the Food and Drug Administration, which directs biomedical research, to the private sector multinational pharmaceutical industry, and the mass media. ACT UP has become one of the most remarkable and successful political forces in modern America, drawing on a long tradition of carefully organised civil disobedience, to which it adds the skills and techniques of modern advertising and video technology.[28] It has also drawn together the various constituencies of race, class and sexuality affected by the epidemic, into the new social identity of the committed AIDS activist. ACT UP was able to draw on an extraordinary flourishing of networks of medical and welfare-related information that had emerged in the mid-1980s, providing gay men in particular with details concerning all aspects of the epidemic that they were systematically denied from other sources. Most remarkable of these has been the continuing literature concerning biomedical research and the ethics of clinical trials, in relation both to private medicine and the state. From very early on it was recognised in the USA that AIDS is through and through a *political* issue, and that no major decisions are made about any aspect of the epidemic that are not informed by economic and ideological priorities, rather than the health and welfare of people with HIV.

Given the close links between British and American gay culture, it is surprising that such understandings have been far less developed in the UK, or elsewhere in Europe. This confirms the point that throughout the EC, people with HIV in countries with socialised medicine tend to have a far less critical attitude to their doctors, and have much greater faith that the overall goals of medical research will not conflict with their own personal interests. In a European context, the demands of ACT UP that people with HIV should be consulted at every stage in the design of protocols for clinical trials implies a much more active model of involvement in the power of relations of medicine, and a more immediately political perception of those same relations. The insistence that clinical trials of new drugs should be regarded as forms of treatment is a radical threat to the traditional divisions between 'pure' researchers and primary care physicians. This has been most marked in the emergence of Community Research Initiatives (CRI), which have mushroomed in the United States in recent years, though not without considerable resistance from the medical establishment.

Practices of Freedom

The CRI movement insists that biomedical research should take place in the community, with general practitioners providing counselling, support and constant monitoring for those who have volunteered to take part in such experimental trials. This has had the great advantage of permitting large numbers of fast, clinical trials in an emergency situation, and has gone some way to challenge the standard procedural use of placebos which, it is objected, literally *require* that many people will sicken and die in the course of 'successful' experiments. This new focus on medical ethics on the part of the communities affected by AIDS marks a profound break in the history of modern pathological medicine, and it is significant that it has been the gay community which *forced* such major innovations.

Unfortunately the situation in Britain is unlikely to produce such dramatic and far-reaching changes in the practice of medicine, if only because gay men here have largely lacked the support of strong advocacy organisations like the American Civil Liberties Union (ACLU) and others, which have played an important role at all levels of the US epidemic, from fighting direct discrimination through the courts, to championing patients' rights in relation to biomedical research. Furthermore, the British Left which might have been expected to take an active interest in the epidemic has on the contrary largely ignored it. Sadly, we suffer from the long legacy of a tradition of ultra-leftism that seems trapped in its own estimations of radicalism that rarely exceed the field of class-related politics, which is hopelessly inadequate to the complexities of power in the modern world. This is not of course to deny the centrality of class in British society, but to point out the impossibility of trying to understand or intervene in the political struggles around AIDS in class terms alone. Moreover, the Left generally chooses to interpret its refusal or inability to work with other groups and lobbies as evidence of its own purity and correctness, rather than of the bankruptcy of its own self-styled radicalism. A similar puritanical separatism also afflicts many sections of the British women's movement, which has still hardly begun to grasp the wider political significance of AIDS, in relation to longstanding concerns about the management of sexuality and sexual reproduction. At a further extreme, 'revolutionary' feminists have long seen AIDS in terms that differ little from those of *The Sun* or *The News of the World*: as a condition that only affects

175

'the enemy', that is men, and women who collude with them.

The history of the British AIDS epidemic demonstrates with disturbing clarity that lesbians and gay men are still far from widely recognised as a legitimate social consituency within British society, or that we continue to face a health crisis unparalleled in modern times. When Health Minister David Mellor observed that perhaps 25 per cent of gay men in London may already be infected, his only comment was that 'people must not breathe a sigh of relief and think it will soon blow over'.[29] Such statements betray a shocking indifference to the actual scale of suffering caused by HIV – shocking, but hardly surprising given the generally abysmal record of British journalism outside the gay press since the very beginning of the epidemic. The mass media continue to pump out prejudice and misinformation that either confuses and alarms readers, or simply denies any possibilty of risk to 'decent' people. We may fairly detect two consistent characteristics of such attitudes. On the one hand, the presentation of AIDS as a 'gay plague' continues to articulate deep anxieties about homosexuality. The epidemic thus becomes the viral projection of an unconscious desire to kill gay men, and these unconscious attitudes should never be discounted or underestimated.[30] On the other hand, the 'homosexualising' of AIDS, and the denial of HIV transmission among heterosexuals offers a semi-magical delusion of intrinsic safety which is as potentially threatening to heterosexuals, as their homophobia is to gay men.[31]

In all this, it should be apparent that fundamental questions about the meaning of democracy in modern Britain are at stake. We should not have to struggle against the odds to establish effective health education which rejects scare-mongering, victim-blaming, and irrational sexual puritanism. Effective health education should be a basic and indisputable right, and never more so than during an epidemic. At the same time, standards of health-care provision and medical research should never be dependent upon the individual's sexuality, class, race or ethnicity. The political management of the British AIDS epidemic demonstrates repeatedly and at all levels that there are many higher priorities than either preventive medicine or the saving of lives. It is therefore critically important that we should be able to identify the leading institutions responsible for deciding and directing social policies in relation to HIV disease, from individual departments of government, to the mass media, regional and district health authorities, the Health Education Authority, the General Medical Council and so on, in order to lobby them effectively. If such institutions fail to respond, civil disobedience may well prove necessary, and ACT UP (London), which was formed early in 1989, has already organised a number of well-targeted demonstrations in relation to the cut-backs in social security and other issues.

Unfortunately, ACT UP faces formidable problems in Britain. Firstly, there are the difficulties of 'band-waggoning' and attempts to hijack the emergent AIDS activist movement by far-left 'interventionists'. Secondly, there is no sustained tradition of civil disobedience politics in Britain, and British police definitely do not recognise lesbians and gay men as a legitimate social constituency, unlike many other European countries. Similarly there is no local tradition of training in non-violent civil disobedience, or of the organisation of 'affinity groups' which has been so successful in ACT UP (New York) – establishing small, close networks of people who have prepared before a given action to work as a team. Thirdly, there is little sense in Britain of the possible role of a cultural politics concerned with images and symbols, such as exists in the USA, where the famous 'Silence = Death' poster from 1986 opened the way for a whole flood of incisive and stylish political posters, T-shirts, badges, which provide AIDS activists with a strong cultural identity, and which in turn have raised vital issues of information in the public spaces of New York. Lastly, the absence of the sense of constitutional rights that so shapes American oppositional politics makes demonstrators very vulnerable to arbitrary arrest and violence, and means that there is not a large and 'ready-made' culture of direct political interventionism on which to draw. This was reflected in the early decision by the 'Frontliners' organisation, which works on behalf of people with AIDS, to dissociate totally itself from ACT UP (London), on the bizarre grounds that:

Certain extreme elements ... have called for demonstrations which would result in people with AIDS/ARC and people with disabilities being arrested.[32]

Clearly the author of that comment could not imagine a situation in which people with AIDS might decide for themselves whether or not they wanted to take part in organised civil disobedience. Nor do British AIDS service organisations appreciate the full extent to which the influence of ACT UP (New York) and other AIDS activist groups such as AIDS Action Now (Toronto) is *already* being felt in UK. For example, the Bristol-Myers corporation has announced plans to make the anti-HIV drug DDI available on the grounds of 'compassionate usage' largely as a result of North American activist pressure. Bristol-Myers have also been careful to include members of AIDS service organisations and the gay press at planning and information meetings, which is unheard of in the field of British pharmaceutical industry behaviour.

It is clear then that AIDS can generate political identities which did not precede the epidemic, and draw together groups such as lesbians and gay men, together with black people and the disabled in ways that could not have been anticipated before the AIDS crisis. Such identities and alliances are not natural or inevitable, but have to be forged in collective experience and in shared aims and objectives. For those like myself, who have had direct long-term experience of the American HIV epidemic, personal loss has been a major motivating factor in our personal involvement. But this is clearly not the case for most lesbians and gay men in the UK, who are still statistically unlikely to have knowingly had much direct experiences of HIV disease, especially outside London. At the same time it is abundantly clear from the consistently low rates of new cases of HIV infection among gay men since 1984 that it has *not* been direct experience of AIDS that has determined the success of the Safer Sex revolution in our lives, or the extraordinary growth of non-governmental AIDS service organisations all round the country. On the contrary, it has been the strength of gay culture – from the gay press to theatre and independent film, but most of all in our everyday lives and friendships.

Yet it is precisely gay culture that the present government has consistently targetted, and that the opposition seems unwilling or unable to defend. We constantly hear that straight society has nothing to learn from us, that we are an 'exceptional' case, that we only took up Safer Sex when we literally saw our friends and lovers dying in front of our very eyes. Such an interpretation is not only ignorant and insulting, it is also profoundly tragic, for it strongly suggests that anti-gay prejudice will continue to prevent many heterosexuals from even trying to learn from our collective cultural experience. This is why the question of entitlement to effective community-based health education and health-care provision, especially in the form of community medicine, is so apparent to so many lesbians and gay men, especially since we are rarely, if ever, identified as a community of need by the National Health Service and other state institutions, regardless of the specific needs relating to AIDS.

In the short term it is increasingly important for lesbians and gay men to develop effective lobbying organisations at Westminster and Brussels. It is also vital that we should continue to build on the new solidarity that we have forged in resistance to Clause 28, throughout the UK. Yet our resources are very limited, and the many tasks of HIV/AIDS work, from distracting fund-raising to direct service provision, are often all but overwhelming (even though these are still the early years of the British epidemic). The experience of AIDS has raised fundamental questions for lesbians and gay men alike concerning the workings of British politics: it is far from clear that we can ever expect British parliamentarianism to recognise our demands for civil rights across a wide range of institutions from the age of consent laws, to health care and education at all levels, and to party politics themselves. At a time when any mention of advocacy for gay people is dismissed as an electoral 'liability', it is hard not to conclude that we ourselves are regarded in a similar light. For it is precisely the fossilised forms and unquestioned values of parliamentary procedure and tradition that have guaranteed many aspects of otherwise wholly avoidable suffering and stress for people with HIV, their families and communities. In housing, social security provision, life insurance, health promotion, treatment research and direct health-care provision, it is painfully apparent that we are not regarded as political subjects with the same rights as other holders of British passports, even in the circumstances of a health crisis that has affected us far more seriously than any other section of the overall population.

179

Conclusion: Practices of Freedom

The long domination of the United Kingdom by England and effectively Westminster has meant that we have never established the range of progressive, federalised national or state identities that have proved so important as the prerequisite for gay political and cultural recognition in countries such as Canada, Australia, the USA, or in the Scandinavian League. Instead we are stuck with relatively conservative nationalist movements and parties that are generally insensitive to feminism and sexual politics. In these circumstances we cannot rely on the assumption that lesbians and gay men will be able to establish autonomous 'gay rights' in advance of other major *constitutional* reforms that are essential for any enlargement of British working democracy and democratic pluralism. At a time when pluralism is itself such a distinctly unfashionable concept, on the grounds of its 'moral relativisim', it is worth considering Josef Brodsky's timely reminder that 'moral absolutism is not so hot either'.[33] This suggests a shift away from a sexual politics founded on the theory of discrete 'minorities', each with an attached bundle of specific rights, towards a far more adventurous vision of democratic politics – the wider context of full citizenship, guaranteed by a Bill of Rights. This involves a direct refusal of the status of subjecthood and the subjectivities it produces, as well as the entire political culture of parliamentary hierarchy and deference that leaves us all subject to the whim of any government that has managed to achieve the absolute power of a parliamentary majority.

Substantial numbers of British lesbians and gay men who have hitherto lacked much sense of a collective identity are now waking up to the direct realities of discrimination and culturally sanctioned prejudice. The deeply engrained sexual conservatism of the labour movement in Britain has effectively abandoned radical sexual politics to the far Left and the women's movement, neither of which have any direct relation to the lives of most gay men. This in effect means that many lesbians and gay men tend to associate the very notion of 'rights' with larger political programmes with which they have little sympathy. At the same time, an articulate but numerically tiny core of professional lobbyists continues a politics in and around the palace of Westminster that has hardly changed since the long years of lobbying that preceded and followed the publication of the Wolfenden Report on homosexual law reform in 1957 – in many cases they are the same people. But the assimilationist approach offers few if any real opportunities for the establishment of a broadly-based and effective gay politics in the foreseeable future, for the obvious reason that such an approach is so deeply committed to the parliamentary status quo.

We urgently need to establish a far more ethically grounded politics of gender and sexuality, in order to realise what Michel Foucault described in one of his final interviews as 'practices of freedom': 'For what', he asked 'is morality, if not the practice of liberty, the deliberate practice of liberty?'[34] Rather than assuming a natural, inevitable unity among gay men, or between gay men and lesbians, such an approach grounds our experience, in all its diversity and complexity, within a wider *ethical* context. We need to ensure, constitutionally, that no other social constituencies will ever have to endure what gay men have been through in increasing numbers throughout the course of the 1980s, as if *our* health and *our* lives are not as irreducibly valuable as those of other sections of society. The concept and practice of citizenship is one powerful means to this end precisely because citizenship not only involves a discourse of rights, but also of *responsibilities*. Without such a double emphasis, pluralism quickly descends into a free-for-all competition between rival and conflicting definitions of rights and difference becomes an identity to be defended by a siege mentality that obscures shared patterns of oppression. AIDS has demonstrated with frightening clarity that lesbians and gay men are not just under-represented within the existing framework of British politics, but are positively excluded from the most basic processes and practices of democracy. This sordid reality has been tacitly or 'tactically' accepted for far too long.

Subjecthood .remains the dominant British political identity, founded in the constitutional settlement of 1688. As such, it has protected British politics from what has long been regarded by Westminster as the threat of federalism. It is the ideological cement that holds together the fragile unity of the United Kingdom, but is increasingly vulnerable to the critiques both of competing nationalisms, and the more general cultural pressures that lie behind the emergence of the 'new social movements' of feminism, black politics, environmentalism and gay liberation. Over time, subjecthood has also served to defend the claims and privileges of parliamentarianism, providing a transcendent national political identity, united in allegiance to the Crown-in-parliament, over and above the divisions of class and all other structures of social difference. Furthermore, it encourages the belief that any criticism of either parliamentarianism or the monarchy itself are somehow 'unpatriotic' and anti-democratic. Subjecthood is thus intimately connected to the wider patterns of cultural and class-based deference that are so characteristic of British politics and civil society, by comparison with other European nations.

A whole bundle of major constitutional reforms have recently come under discussion in the wake of the publication of Charter 88. These include electoral reform, freedom of information legislation, the formal incorporation into British law of the European Convention for the Protection of Human Rights and Fundamental Freedoms, a Bill of Rights, the reform of the judicary and so on. What is now needed is an energetic *ideological* initiative, to recruit support for these concrete issues of entitlements and responsibilities as they arise for different social constituencies. In its current formulation, the movement for constitutional change in Britain retains the primacy of political and legal institutions which would be empowered to endow or deny rights with the same impunity as the parliamentary traditions that Charter 88 seems unwilling to challenge adequately. This explains the importance of emphasising the *ethical* dimensions of political and legal reform programmes, and of holding on to questions of power in relation to identiy, which is especially important if we accept that identity is not a simple, unitary, and uniformly consistent entity, given from birth. The political culture of subjecthood involves a clear ranking of priorities within our individual and collective identities, a *subjection* to political, juridical and regal authority in our sense of who we are. Citizenship, however, at least offers the potential for very different processes of identification with one another, founded upon ethical considerations that should always be understood to have precedence and priority over the domain of the legal and the political.

Citizenship emerges as one strategy in what Foucault described as the 'political technology of individuals',[35] who may be brought to recognise and identify themselves through many different aspects and arenas of the social formation, whether through gender, nationalism, religion, health issues, regionalism, race and so on. In one of his later lectures Foucault described his aim to

> show people that a lot of things that are a part of their landscape – that people think are universal – are the result of some very precise historical changes. All my analyses are against the idea of universal necessities in human existence. They show the arbitrariness of institutions and show which space of freedom we can still enjoy and how many changes can still be made.[36]

This is especially obvious in his work concerning the conditions of emergence of the modern categories and identities of sexuality. Much of Foucault's later work was taken up with questions of how such historical understanding might be practically applied, and their ethical implications for the constitution of the sense of self. From this perspective, citizenship also offers a concrete alternative to the type of humanism

> that presents a certain form of ethics as a universal model for any kind of freedom. I think there are more secrets, more possible freedoms, and more inventions in our future than we can imagine in humanism as it is dogmatically represented in every side of the political rainbow.[37]

This is in itself hardly surprising, since humanism has a prior interest in arguing that identity precedes social and political structures, which are seen to work in a purely external way upon a pre-formed rational 'human' subject, which is incompatible with Foucault's contention that:

> In effect, we live in a legal, social, and institutional world where the only relations possible are extremely few, extremely simplified, and extremely poor ... Society and the institutions that frame it have limited the possibility of relationships because a rich relational world would be very complex to manage. We should fight against this shrinking of the relational fabric.[38]

The concept of citizenship naturally develops from his interest in the notion of relational rights that might supplant both the given power relations of sexuality and gender relations, and the excessive claims made by the modern state over our affectional lives. His argument lends great weight to our contemporary need to find ways to acknowledge personal relations beyond the current cultural validation of marriage and the family, as if these exhausted the possibilities of legitimate social and sexual choice.

One great weakness in the discourse of civil rights in Britain has been its long association with minorities, as if rights were not fundamental for the entire population. Entitlements have similarly been widely regarded primarily as *exemptions*, such as council housing, free prescriptions, or free school meals, thus limiting the concept to the weak and the disadvantaged. An ethically grounded practice of citizenship has the great initial advantage of being posed to, and on behalf of, the entire population – no longer pictured in crude parliamentary terms as a majority surrounded on all sides by distinct and possibly threatening minorities, but rather as a complex unity of many overlapping and interrelated groups and identities. Citizenship invites such a politics that proceeds from the recognition that our identities are multiply formed and positioned, rather than fixed rigidly in mechanical dualistic polarities.

Ten long years of Thatcherism have brought home to many the full significance of Foucault's stark observation that:

> The search for a form of morality that would be acceptable for everyone – in the sense that everyone would have to submit to it – strikes me as catastrophic.[39]

It is precisely from our close understanding of the catastrophe to which such a search has led us that the recognition of the need for a common goal of ethical citizenship emerges, and with it the conditions for the emergence of new political identities and forms of social solidarity. In this respect, ethical citizenship anticipates Hannah Arendt's political vision of *the republic*, dedicated to the overriding principle of *freedom*, that is quite distinct from familiar notions of popular sovereignty. For Arendt, freedom is incompatible with the democratic politics of majority rule, which ensure that minorities are inevitably oppressed. In her political vision, modern western democracies are at best a 'very imperfect realisation' of the ideal of the free commonwealth, embodied readily in the

184

corresponding concept of *citizenship*.[40] The political history of the AIDS epidemic strongly supports Arendt's explanation of the origins of totalitarianism, which insists that totalising state power starts

> with *the story of the pariah*, and therefore with the 'exception', with the 'politically anomolous' which is then used to explain the rest of society, rather than the other way round.[41]

The experience of countries such as France, West Germany and the United States demonstrates that the status of legal citizenship does not of itself automatically curb excessive state power or the oppression of minorities. But such countries do enjoy the benefits of the *culture of citizenship* that are almost entirely absent from the UK, where the concept of national sovereignty so frequently steamrollers any respect for cultural diversity within the nation. In this light, citizenship emerges not simply as a political goal, but both as an ethical necessity, in defence of old liberties and as a means for the active encouragement of new practices of freedom, on which the very possibility of a future for Britain as a fully European democracy currently depend.

Notes

[1] Charter 88, London 1988.

[2] Stuart Hall and David Held, 'Left and Rights', *Marxism Today*, June 1989, pp16-17.

[3] Douglas Crimp, 'Mourning and Militancy', *October* (forthcoming, 1990).

[4] See Simon Watney, 'Introduction', in Erica Carter and Simon Watney (eds), *Taking Liberties: AIDS and Cultural Politics*, Serpent's Tail, London 1989.

[5] Raymond Williams, *Towards 2000*, Chatto & Windus, London 1983, p.107-8.

[6] Michael Elliott, 'Constitutionalism, Sovereignty and Politics', in Richard Holme and Michael Elliott (eds) *1688-1988: Time For A New Constitution*, Macmillan, Basingstoke 1988, p26.

[7] *Ibid.*, p30.

[8] See Simon Watney, *op.cit.*

[9] See Stuart Hall, *Thatcherism and the Crisis of the Left: The Hard Road To Renewal*, Verso, London 1988.

[10] Karl Marx, 'Theses on Feuerbach', in Karl Marx, and Frederick Engels, *The German Ideology*, International Publishers, New York 1967, p199.

[11] See Larry Gostin, 'Towards Resolving The Conflicts', in Larry Gostin, (ed), *Civil Liberties in Conflict*, Routledge, London 1988, pp7-21.

[12] Raymond Williams, *op.cit.*, pp250-1.

[13] Simon Watney, *op.cit.*, pp25-6.

[14] David Marquand, 'Citizenship', *Analysis*, BBC Radio Four, 29 March 1989.

[15] Paul Nettleton, 'Hattersley says PR reduces democracy', *The Guardian*, 6 October 1989.

[16] *Ibid.*

[17] Raymond Williams, *op.cit.*, pp109-10.

[18] Ralf Dahrendorf, 'Citizenship and the Modern Social Conflict', in Richard Holme and Michael Elliott, *op.cit.*, p113.

[19] *Ibid.*, pp114-5.

[20] *Ibid.*, p116.

[21] Raymond Williams *op.cit.* p123.

[22] John Jackson, 'Age of consent', *The Guardian*, 4 October 1989.

[23] Douglas Crimp, *op.cit.*

[24] See Simon Watney, *op.cit.*

[25] Medical Research Council, *AIDS Directed Programme: Programme Plan and Research Opportunities*, London, July 1988.

[26] See Simon Watney, 'Tasks in AIDS Research', *Gay Times*, May 1989.

[27] Quoted in Douglas Crimp, 'AIDS: Cultural Analysis/Cultural Activism' in Douglas Crimp (ed), *AIDS: Cultural Analysis/Cultural Activism*, MIT Press, Cambridge Mass. 1988, p11.

[28] See Simon Watney, 'Representing AIDS' in Sunil Gupta (ed), *Ecstatic Antibodies*, Arts Council/Rivers Oram Press, London 1990.

[29] *Daily Mirror*, 4 October 1988.

[30] See Simon Watney, 'The Possibilities of Permutation: Pleasure, Proliferation and the Politics of Gay Identity in the Age of AIDS' in James Miller (ed), *AIDS: Crisis and Criticism*. University of Toronto Press, Toronto 1990.

[31] See Simon Watney, 'Safer Sex as Community Practice' in Peter Aggleton *et al* (eds), *AIDS: Individual, Cultural and Policy Dimensions*, Falmer Press, Lewes 1990.

[32] 'Frontliners disassociation from ACT UP', *Frontiers*, No. 4, 1 June 1989.

[33] Josef Brodsky, 'Isaiah Berlin at Eighty', *The New York Review of Books*, 17 August 1989.

[34] Michel Foucault, 'The Ethic of Care for the Self as a Practice of Freedom' in James Bernauer and David Rasmussen (eds), *The Final Foucault*, MIT Press, Cambridge Mass. 1988, p4.

[35] Michel Foucault, 'Truth, Power, Self: An Interview' in Martin L. Luther *et al* (eds), *Technologies of the Self: A Seminar with Michel Foucault*, Tavistock, London 1988.

[36] *Ibid.*, p11.

[37] *Ibid.*, p15.

[38] Michel Foucault, 'The Social Triumph of the Sexual Will', *Christopher Street*, Issue 64, Vol, 6, No. 4, New York 1982, p38.

[39]Michel Foucault, 'The Return of Morality' in Sylvère Lotringer (ed), *Foucault Live*, Semiotext(e), New York 1989, p330.
[40]Agnes Heller and Ferenc Feher, *The Postmodern Political Condition*, Polity Press, London 1989, p97.
[41]*Ibid.*, p89.

A Nasty Piece of Work: A Psychoanalytic Study of Sexual and Racial Difference in 'Mona Lisa'

LOLA YOUNG

Both authorised and anecdotal literature have created too many stories about Negroes to be suppressed. But putting them all together does not help us in our real task, which is to disclose their mechanics. What matters for us is not to collect facts and behaviour, but to find their meaning.

Frantz Fanon, *Black Skin, White Masks*

Frantz Fanon, the Black psychiatrist who fought for Algeria's liberation from French rule, wrote in France in the early 1950s that 'if one wants to understand the racial situation psychoanalytically ... as it is experienced by individual consciousness, considerable importance must be given to sexual phenomena'.[1] Sexual relationships between Black and White people are frequently alluded to but rarely openly discussed: even today the subject arouses fierce debate and controversy in both Black and White communities. It seems that inter-racial sexuality is the unmentionable act in the context of a racist society. The avoidance of meaningful discussions about such relationships generally is underlined by the prohibitions associated with inter-racial sexuality on film. How might we use psychoanalysis to unravel the relationship between sex and 'race' on film? And if it is true, as has been argued, that a racist society will have a racist science,[2] is there any potential for the productive use of psychoanalysis to describe and explain racism?

Like Fanon, I believe that psychoanalytic theory has a significant contribution to make to the understanding of the psychic processes involved in the construction of racism and racist ideologies, and thus to their dismantling. In order to explore the possibilities of a fruitful alliance between psychoanalysis and anti-racism, I should like to look at some aspects of the development of the human psyche using psychoanalytic terms.

In attempting to use psychoanalytic theory to reveal the psychic mechanisms involved in the construction of racial difference, I am aware of some contradictions. Freud's challenge to the ideology of liberal-humanism through the decentring of the subject from its pivotal position – the omniscient 'bourgeois' individual – has been described as revolutionary. However, some of the uses to which psychoanalysis has been put have not fulfilled its radical potential. Psychoanalysis has frequently been appropriated as an instrument of repression, and rehabilitation into social conformity, by the dominant forms of Western psychotherapeutic practice, and there is certainly enough evidence to suggest that many institutional procedures have oppressed Black people in a number of ways.[3] Also, even though Freud maintained that the phenomena he described were transcultural, ubiquitous experiences, psychoanalysis has often been criticised as a set of culturally and temporally specific observations and extrapolations which have acquired the status of a universal theory. As a result, this has led to a tendency to dismiss psychoanalysis as eurocentric and ahistorical, and thus of no use to Black people.

Yet Fanon found much that was useful, especially in the description of White people's fantasies about Black people. His book *Black Skin, White Masks* (first published in 1952) was primarily concerned with the feelings of inadequacy and inferiority to which Blacks were prone under colonial rule and he used psychoanalysis and psychology to describe and explain the effects of colonisation and oppression on the Black psyche. Fanon proposed a two-part study containing both a 'psychoanalytic interpretation of the life experience of the Black man' and a 'psychoanalytic interpretation of the Negro myth'.[4] However, progress in understanding the deep structures of the mind which contribute to the perpetuation of racism has been slow: Fanon's questions and the issues he raised have direct relevance to the way in which we conceptualise our positions in British society today. Because the understanding of a single instance in some detail can facilitate the understanding of many similar instances, I want to take the film 'Mona Lisa' (directed by Neil Jordan in 1986) as a representative illustration of a general ideological condition.

There are several reasons for looking at this particular product of the British film industry. 'Mona Lisa' is intriguing because it illustrates the ways in which issues of race may circulate in a text without being made explicit through a strong Black presence: one of the absorbing elements of the film is that although it is imbued with 'race', it continually refuses to engage with the racial issues raised. 'Mona Lisa' is also noteworthy for its combined use of racial, class and sexual difference as signifiers of threat and disorder. To study a specific problem – that is, the conjunction of racial and sexual difference – the form, content and style of contemporary cultural products provide a framework for the discussion of current attitudes. The film is all the more interesting as it was an international and domestic success, winning several prestigious awards and almost unanimous critical acclaim.

The film's narrative is centred on the rather dense George (Bob Hoskins), recently released from prison, and his developing relationship with Black prostitute Simone (Cathy Tyson). George is hired by the objectionable Mortwell (Michael Caine) – a former colleague who owes George a favour – to deliver pornographic videos and drive Simone to and from her rich clients. Initially, there is much antagonism between the tasteless, sporadically violent George and the aloof, expensively dressed Simone but as the story progresses, George becomes emotionally attached to her and agrees to search for her drug-addicted young friend Cathy (Kate Hardie), also a prostitute. George locates and then abducts Cathy and subsequently flees with her and Simone to Brighton. There he learns that Simone and Cathy are lovers; he is clearly devastated by what he perceives as Simone's betrayal of his emotions. The abduction and flight angers Mortwell who is running the vice network for which both Simone and Cathy work and he pursues the three fugitives. Accompanying Mortwell is the brutal Anderson

(Clarke Peters), Simone's former and Cathy's present pimp. Simone shoots Mortwell and Anderson and is about to shoot George when he grabs her hand with the gun pointed at him. The final scene shows George reconciled with his estranged teenage daughter (Zoe Nathenson) and his eccentric friend Thomas (Robbie Coltrane) working and walking together as one contented 'family' unit.

Racist Mindsets

In the USA, during the late 1960s, it was Black Power activist Stokeley Carmichael who advised White psychologists, that they should 'stop investigating and examining people of colour, they ought to investigate and examine their own corrupt society'.[5] Joel Kovel took up the challenge issued by Carmichael, writing *White Racism: A Psychohistory* which was first published in 1970. In it, Kovel describes two main types of racist: the dominative racist who acts out her or his supermacist beliefs with the overt intention of subjugating Blacks; and the aversive racist.[6]

Kovel's formulation of aversive racism echoes Fanon's description of Blacks as a stimulus to anxiety in White people. Most Black people will have observed and experienced as Fanon did, White people's feelings of revulsion prompted by actual or potential physical contact with Blacks. The aversive racist is a complex 'ideal type' according to Kovel and may indulge in a range of feelings and actions which vary in intensity and level of development. If an aversive racist perceives a threat from Blacks because they are getting too close – too many moving into a neighbourhood or frequent socialising with young White people – action, motivated by belief in White superiority, will follow.

However, it may be the case that, inspired by liberal or socialist principles or social conscience, the aversive racist will be found working to ameliorate intolerable housing conditions, drug addiction and so on amongst Blacks. Crucially though, the desire to improve the fabric of Black people's lives manifests itself through involvement in social reform by the most remote means available, avoiding actual proximity with Blacks as far as possible. Disconcertingly, aversive racists frequently appear 'liberal' and 'tolerant', seemingly supporting struggles for Black liberation: yet

191

beneath this veneer of 'ideologically correct' activity, they maintain the features of aversion.

A current example of this is that in conversations with a number of Whites, it has become apparent that there is often a subtext to arguments about moving from the big city into the countryside. The discussion usually centres on the supposed improved quality of life: it is cleaner and less violent there, the children will get a better education and so on. These constitute the stated reasons for the move. Crucially though, Black communities are virtually non-existent in rural areas. This frequently 'hidden agenda' is implicit in 'Mona Lisa': there is the consistent association of the presence of Blacks with the lowering of standards, with garbage and with outbreaks of violence and illicit sexual activity. Black people's 'extreme' behaviour such as uprisings, criminal activity and so forth, force the aversive individual to respond with more or less covert expressions of 'race' hatred.

Avoiding issues raised by inter-racial sexual relationships and maintaining a distance from any activity which may be interpreted as inter-racial intimacy on anything other than a superficial level are amongst the strategies of aversion. A consistent feature of films written and directed by Whites is a refusal to relate intimately to Black people's knowledge and experiences, despite protestations to the contrary. This is most obviously evidenced by the continuing absence of significant Black characters in contemporary settings and the frequent refuge taken in the production of period pieces where, in their ignorance, White writers and directors with seemingly impeccable liberal credentials still seem unable to grasp the essential point: Black people live and die in this country, undergoing a full spectrum of emotional experiences and have done so for several hundred years. Given the creative opportunities afforded by a culturally diverse society and the potential for depicting the diversity of our experiences, the practice of aversive racism may be seen as a significant feature of British mainstream and 'art' cinema and thus, 'distance becomes a singularly effective mode of defensive adaptation'.[7] This distancing is illustrated in 'Mona Lisa' in interviews given by Neil Jordan and David Leland (who wrote the screenplay), Cathy Tyson – the Black actress who played the female lead role of prostitute – was praised for her ability *not* to appear too sexually attractive. As Neil Jordan states, 'It's an anti-erotic movie ... we were helped by the casting of Cathy Tyson, because she's so angular and strong. She's also rather beautiful but you don't necessarily think of her sexiness.'[8] It is a comment that indicates the adoption of a strategy of remoteness and distancing from the Black female subject and her sexuality which is a necessary corollary of the fear, anxiety and disgust mentioned earlier.

Blacks are constantly constituted by Whites as 'the fantasy of a fantasy – not cold, pure, clean, efficient, industrious, frugal, rational (that is, not the pantheon of anal-negative ego traits which are the *summum bonum* of the bourgeois order) but rather warm, dirty, sloppy, feckless, lazy, improvident and irrational, all those traits that are associated with Blackness, odor, and sensuality ...'.[9] For Whites to see themselves as rational, ordered and civilised people, they have to construct a notion of irrationality, disorder and uncivilised behaviour which is then imposed on the object of their stimulus to anxiety. Elements of the culture which are repressed re-emerge in the despised culture. So that where Whites may have fantasies about total sexual abandonment whilst living under a yoke of sexual repression, that fantasy is projected onto Blacks. The Black woman is sexualised, objectified and associated with both the primal and the inappropriately over-civilised – the latter signified in 'Mona Lisa' through Simone's use of stockings, corsets and whips and so on – whilst being designated the origin of perverse forms of sexual behaviour. Simone is wide-eyed in her gazes at George, at times assuming the role of the 'unconsciously sexualised exotic',[10] the child-like Black, at the same time as being sexually knowing and aware. This is part of a fantasy constructed by White male writers of what characterises Black female sexuality. As Gilman points out 'It is indeed the pure child as sexual object, the child free from the curse of adult sexuality ... which is projected onto the exotic as sexual object'.[11]

In Freudian psychoanalytic terms, projection describes the process whereby the subject attributes the intolerable passions and inclinations – intolerable because considered to be manifestations of the 'bad' self – to others that she or he is unable to accept in her – or himself. Thus the racist will project her or his own fears and disposition on to the despised racial group. Near the beginning of

Identity

'Mona Lisa', George asks his friend Thomas, after he has been emphatically rejected by his wife, 'where did they all come from?', referring to the Black people who have just witnessed one of his violent outbursts. The question which might be legitimately asked of George is, 'where has *he* come from?' He has been in prison for seven years: now he returns home expecting a hero's welcome and for things to be just as they were before he was sent down. His own feelings of inadequacy and guilt are projected onto the Blacks who are instantly designated as 'other', encroaching on 'his' territory.

Within the cultural framework which sustains this construction of Blacks, White is a non-category. English Whites in general are unused to regarding themselves as members of ethnic groups or as having an ethnic identity beyond that of being superior in relation to other ethnic groups. White is the norm against which everything else is measured, and it has no need of self-definition. Part of the success of 'Whiteness' is that most of the time it does not appear to exist at all.[12]

The Discourse of 'Race'

The subordination of Black people is frequently based on commonsense notions of 'race' informed by supposed psychological, physical and intellectual characteristics, and derived from the spurious notions of scientific and anthropological research, such as those demonstrated in eighteenth-and nineteenth-century pseudo-scientific racism and 'eugenics'.

It was believed that each group of people perceived as having different physical characteristics should be considered as different species rather than varieties of the same species. This was a crucial distinction: as if a racial grouping was designated as belonging to a separate species, then it would be assumed that sexual union between the 'races' would be highly undesirable and result in infertile offspring. Theories of natural selection were misappropriated and used to give credence to the belief that the 'superior race' could be transformed to its detriment, by mixing with other 'inferior races'. The allegedly uninhibited physical nature of Black people combined with fears about the mixing of 'races' and served to make the major anxiety stimulated by Blacks a *sexual* one. This

194

anxiety manifested itself in the compulsion to control Black sexuality and fertility, and sexual activity with Whites.

The association of animal imagery with Black people, which is a persistent and recurring feature of eighteenth-century pseudo-scientific racism, also echoes in 'Mona Lisa': Simone, the 'tall thin Black tart', describes her former pimp, a Black man named Anderson, as 'an animal born in a butcher's shop'. The association in White popular imagination between Black people and gorillas is invoked in 'Mona Lisa' as George and his friend Thomas watch a video of Simone having oral sex with Anderson. The link between the animalistic images of the two Blacks in the film and sexual deviancy and danger is embedded in the text and interwoven with the image of a voracious, cannibalistic Black woman. During the playing of the video, Thomas remarks 'you used to tell a joke about a randy gorilla'.

As people have come to rely on the phenotypical, differential characteristics of skin colour, hair type and so forth, as constituting the basis for racial classification, so the conflation of Black skins with the negativity of 'Blackness' has become absolute. Extrapolating from visible differences, people use this misrecognition of essential difference as a basis for the expectation of patterns of behaviour in the differentiated group/individual; they relate their expectations to their unconscious psychic needs. The resulting systemic racism is a product of psychological, economic and historical processes and ideological imperatives: 'race' can never be an objective culture-free designation of difference.

The Significance of Difference

In order to understand why difference is important to us and how differentiation becomes racism, it is necessary to understand the process of differentiation in early infancy and its place in the developing human being. According to psychoanalytic theory, in the very early stages of an infant's life, the small baby has no conscious appreciation of itself as itself: it is autoerotic and its undifferentiated body is traversed by a multiplicity of instinctual drives.

The baby's world is initially experienced as an extension of itself and the services rendered to the infant; feeding, warming, comforting and so on are experienced as being that part of the self which is there to satisfy those needs. Once it becomes aware of the difference between itself and the world around it, the infant experiences anxiety as the result of a perception of a loss of control over the fulfilling of its needs and desires. From the moment the infant learns to differentiate between itself and the rest of the world, the notion of what constitutes difference – of 'me-ness' and 'them-ness' – is crucially important to the evolving human psyche.

The anxiety arising from the 'lost' control is repressed by mentally splitting the self and the world-picture of people and objects into 'good' and 'bad'. The 'good' self was originally in control of everything and thus free from anxiety; the 'bad' self has no control over the infant's environment and is prone to suffering apprehension. Contradictions raised by the confrontation between the 'good' and 'bad' facets of the self are painful and difficult to deal with: therefore,

> the 'bad' self is distanced and identified with the mental representation of the 'bad' object … The deep structure of our own sense of self is built upon the illusionary image of the world divided into two camps, 'us' and 'them'. 'They' are either 'good' or 'bad'.[13]

The relationship between the construction of difference and general stereotyping is particularly potent when applied to notions of racial difference predicated on skin colour.

> In 'seeing' (constructing a representational system for) the Other, we search for anatomical signs of difference such as physiognomy and skin color. The Other's physical features, from skin colour to sexual structures such as the shape of the genitalia, are always the antithesis of the idealised self's.[14]

Those who belong to a 'different' people – a people of colour – constitute the Other and are invested with all of the qualities of the 'bad' or, occasionally, the 'good' (as in the myth of the good native, loyal and submissive). But generally Black people come to embody the threat to the illusion of order and control and represent the polar opposite to the White group.

Differences then, are constructed through the process of creating distinct categorisations which assist in the production and maintenance of an illusory order in a chaotic and fragmented world. Thus people who manifestly disturb the boundaries of those categorisations represent a further threat and are doubly problematic. It becomes difficult to pinpoint the qualities which constitute racial and sexual difference if the demarcation lines are blurred: the process and purpose of having differentiated in the first instance are undermined. The anxiety which the creation of the Other was initially intended to alleviate is reactivated and brought to bear on the phobogenic objects: these may often be people defined as 'mixed race' or homosexual.

Having structured the differences into the Other, sexual intermixing becomes an unthinkable, unspeakable act. As the unthinkable cannot be dealt with, the implied danger has to be avoided and aversion is the coping mechanism. Thus, in 'Mona Lisa', in order to ensure that the encounter between George's fantasies of romantic love and the sordid materiality of Simone's lifestyle is never elaborated, various devices are deployed: her sexual performances, both in hotels and on videotape, are used to inform his ultimate alienation from her.[15]

Fears and Loathings

The fear of portraying inter-racial sexual relationships contains within it implicit expressions of fears for the purity and superiority of the White 'race' which, as they relate to 'miscegenation' and 'race-mixing', are evocative of earlier pseudoscientific racist discourse. It is a particularly emotive topic, provoking uneasiness and avoidance, linking back to the old idea that blood varies from 'race' to 'race' and that mixing those bloods is undesirable. The conjunction of 'race' and sex is taboo in a racist society and gives rise to many of the fantasies and myths that White people have about people of African descent. All related language is problematic: 'mulatto', 'half-caste', 'mixed-race', 'inter-racial' and so on.

The character of George in 'Mona Lisa' initially displays a phobic reaction to Black people. As mentioned, earlier, Fanon attempted to explain the psychic processes which foster White experience of Black people as phobogenic, arousing fear and revulsion. Believing that 'anxiety derives from a subjective insecurity linked to the absence of the mother',[16] Fanon points to the endowment of the phobic object with evil intentions, which allows physical contact alone to stimulate (sexual) anxiety. During the opening credits of the film, as George crosses the Thames on his way home, a Black man walks towards him, causing him to do a double take. It is interesting that significance is attached to George's reaction so early in the narrative. He's been in prison for seven years; large-scale immigration from the Caribbean pre-dated the period of his imprisonment by some twenty years. Having lived in South London and been in prison, it is highly unlikely that George would be seeing Black people for the first time. But the instantly identifiable signifier of difference – skin colour – is mobilised to indicate the threat and disorder to come as George re-enacts the shock of Europeans' first encounters with Africans.

In common with other films in which Blacks and Whites appear, the aversion to depicting overtly interracial sexuality is painfully obvious.[17] The potential danger involved in a sexual union across racial lines is averted by characterising Simone as a lesbian. Simone is carefully constructed as a non-sexually threatening character in terms of her relationship to George. Her fertility – which constitutes the ultimate threat that Blacks will reproduce, or mix their blood with Whites thus creating a degenerate, weak 'race' – is contained. Her lesbianism and prostitution mean that her body though useable for sexual gratification is not used for reproductive purposes. The commodification of her sexuality and its control by Mortwell – a White man – recalls the brutal exploitation of Black women's bodies during slavery but it is Anderson's physical violence towards the young White girls that is most often represented. This makes sense within contemporary supremacist ideology which claims that 'race' in a 'biological' sense is not important but that cultures are different. As 'ethnic' groups have different, incompatible value-systems and needs, they are better off separated as conflict will inevitably ensue from attempted integration.

Simone's relationship with her cultural background is concealed and her character has no context in any sense. She is yet another Black character who is 'deracinated' and deprived of her history: although there are a few mentions of her being Black, and of 'niggers' and 'darkies', her reactions to these comments and her utterances do not refer to her sense of self as a Black woman who earns her living by selling sex. She does not seem to acknowledge her existence as a Black prostitute in a dangerous environment. We literally do not know where she's coming from. Who is she? The enigmatic Mona Lisa in the title song sung by Nat King Cole? The only information we are given about her family is that her father beat her as a child. Perhaps this lack of contextualisation is because she is assumed to live in some kind of cultural limbo due to her 'mixed-race' heritage.[18] Her only relationship to other Blacks in the film is brutal and economic. In particular, with Anderson who used to be her pimp, beat her and appeared with her in pornographic videos. Her potential as a Black woman, symbolic of fertility and sexual attraction, is invoked but not realised. The danger signified by all sexualised women is bypassed not only by her 'otherness', but also by the portrayal of all the women as embittered, unco-operative – except through coercion – and unloving towards men.

The anxiety stimulated in men by women's sexuality is especially acute when considered in terms of Black and White social relations for it is here that the threat of its uncontrollability by Whites and its symbolic representation of Black aspirations for liberation from oppression is located. Blackness in itself connotes 'difference': when the subject is also a woman, the difference is reinforced. Simone performs a range of 'deviant' sex often with Black men but has no congress with other Blacks, no visible Black community with whom she may be identified. This stems from the perception that Blacks are most problematic when they gather in groups and prepare for united action. Simone is culturally isolated and this also contributes to her diminution as a real threat to the 'natural' order of White dominance.

The entangled web of pathologised Blacks, working classes, lesbians and prostitutes are a circular construction in the film and in the popular imagination, particularly in relation to the spread of crime, disease and disorder. Simone's identification as sexually 'other' is located in her lesbianism and her rejection of White male sexual identity. This can be understood by appreciating the correlation between 'pathology', 'sexuality' and 'race':

Sexual anatomy is so important a part of self-image that 'sexually different' is tantamount to 'pathological' – the Other is 'impaired', 'sick', 'diseased'. Similarly, physiognomy or skin colour that is perceived as different is immediately associated with 'pathology' and 'sexuality'.[19]

The apparent 'motivation' for Simone's and Cathy's lesbian relationship is the brutality they suffer at the hands of the men who regulate their lives. The possibility that the women might have actually chosen to have a sexual relationship with each other anyway is not allowed, as this would disrupt the relative normality of 'White-on-White' heterosexual relationships: their difference is inscribed as perverse, thus there has to be an 'acceptable' explanation for their 'deviance'.

The narrative serves to pathologise Simone in four areas: as a Black, as a lesbian, as a prostitute and as a woman. The conflation of these four elements is possible because all are constructed through a White male fantasy which sees female genitalia as evidence of an anomalous sexuality and Black female sexuality as a sexual and social threat to be subjected to control. The Black woman is not only the object of sexual perversity, she is also its source. Alongside that, the belief that female prostitution is somehow a natural consequence of excessive female sexuality still has currency: in film narratives virtually any active female sexuality is likely to be conflated, at least symbolically, with prostitution. In both medical and legal discourse, the pubescent female is seen as sexually threatening and liable to bring about her own destruction. In 'Mona Lisa', the youth of the prostitutes he sees allows George to experience guilt-free concern over the sexual maturation of his daughter, even though he left his family to look after themselves for the years he was imprisoned. In the scenes where he goes to pick up his teenage daughter from school, he 'kerb-crawls' along the route she takes home and invites her into the car: these scenes parallel the way in which the girls looking for trade in King's Cross enter the cars of their prospective clients. In fact the men appear to view prostitution as the natural development for the female child, and give themselves permission to punish the women relentlessly for their supposed failure to satisfy other men. The pimps have a dual role though, because at the same time as beating the girls, they are there to 'protect' them: and George is there to save them and make 'honest' women out of them.

The function of the portrayal of male violence – particularly, but

200

A Nasty Piece of Work

not exclusively exemplified by the Black pimp Anderson – is to use
these men as examples of 'otherness'. Thus the character of George,
the character who invites 'us' to identify with him,[20] is exempted
from being judged as an instigator of unjustified 'bad' acts. His
outbursts of violence, if sometimes excessive are nonetheless
vindicated as a reaction to provocation. We are discouraged from
criticising his violent behaviour on the same level as the other men.
The splitting off of George's 'bad' self and its projection onto other
men is convenient, allowing as it does, the continued self-delusion of
him being a fully integrated, rational personality: when we reach the
point in the film where Simone shoots Anderson and Mortwell,
within the world constructed by the narrative, this seems justifiable,
even laudable. The moment she turns on George, any sympathy for
her is negated by the threat she poses to George, the point of
identification. Being able to label her mad, bad and Black induces a
feeling of security in racists – both dominative and aversive – as they
are confirmed in their knowledge of right and wrong, good and bad,
and 'them' and 'not-them'. They are able to reaffirm their sense of
self, secure in the knowledge of being able to identify who is in and
who is outside of their particular community of interest.

The 'Bad' Self

Most White people view Black people through the lens of textual
relationships (by textual I mean cinematic and televisual, as well as
literary) within most texts White is constantly naturalised, so that
Black is non-natural, always different and 'other-wise', at the same
time as being of 'nature' and uninhabited. The actions which Black
characters perform on film do not need explanations or motivations,
as it is assumed that we act on an instinctual level.

Simone's behaviour may be read as markedly pathological since
her perverse and irrational actions towards the end of the film
stigmatise her as being disturbed. This is a familiar motif in the
representation of Black characters in films who often appear to act in
an unmotivated, unpremeditated manner: they represent the
antithesis of White people's control and rationality. The process
whereby Blacks are labelled the mad, irrational people is marked by
the projection of White people's mad, irrational feelings from within

themselves onto the 'other'. Referring again to the initial split which the infant makes between its 'good' and 'bad' self as it becomes aware of objects and people outside of itself, Gilman notes:

> The 'bad' self, with its repressed sadistic impulses, becomes the 'bad' Other; the 'good' self/object, with its infallible correctness, becomes the antithesis to the flawed image of the self, the self out of control. The 'bad' Other becomes the negative stereotype; the 'good' Other becomes the positive stereotype. The former is what we fear to become: the latter that which we cannot achieve.[21]

Like the infant who has to learn to differentiate between itself and the rest of its world, it is as if Britain – as an imperial power – had to discover that its source of comfort, security and warmth did not come from itself but from elsewhere. Similarly, it was and still is a painful experience to have to recognise that the self is not in control and independent but accountable to others and interdependent. Britain was unable to differentiate itself from the rest of *its* world inasmuch as its colonies were part of its sense of self, literally and metaphorically providing food, warmth and comfort. The discovery that the colonies were separate entities with their own demands and needs becomes linked to frustration, loss and anger. The squalor of the once great capital city of the empire, is associated with a crisis in national identity, anxiety is precipitated by loss – loss of control, loss of empire, loss of status as a world power – and the blame is implicitly located in the chaos and disease with which Blacks have contaminated the landscape.

Early in 'Mona Lisa' prior to his arrival at his wife's house, we see George sitting in a park, enjoying a hazy, sunny day: it appears idyllically beautiful, almost a country scene. However, the harsh reality of what most of London has become, at least according to popular belief, returns with a resounding blow. The street where his wife and daughter live, having been 'colonised' by Blacks is punctuated by overflowing rubbish bins and sacks, and signs of decay. Significantly, George's family house is neat with well-stocked hanging baskets, whilst the houses of the Black neighbours are flanked by bags of garbage.

It is significant that several newspaper reviews of the film praised its depiction of London's squalor;[22] the 'deterioration' in the quality of London life is reflected through George's eyes. Even the lush scenes at the Ritz hotel are underscored by the corrupt scenes taking place behind closed doors and the presence of the mainly 'foreign' visitors. London is represented by a world where a sordid, teeming underlife, led by working-class villains and fed on by 'foreigners', is 'in control': a Black pimp ensures the loyalty of his fifteen-year-old prostitutes by beating them and supplying them with hard drugs; the people who stay at the Ritz and use the services that Mortwell runs are Japanese and Arabs.

London's depiction in this film has been described as a 'modern-day Dante's inferno':[23] the scenes in the mythically reconstructed King's Cross with their grotesque population, swirling mists and constant fires are clearly meant to signify some kind of hell. A popular perception is that London's descent into squalor coincided with the influx of settlers from the Caribbean, Africa and Asia. Within the film's fantasy maelstrom of violence, pain, corruption, disorder and unspeakable desire, George is a contemporary evocation of a representative of the 'common man', signifying an innocent, slightly bemused White England from a mythical past.

Cinematic narratives tend to reflect the narratives of the wider world: we can look to 'Mona Lisa' to tell us about some of the perceptions of racial and sexual interaction in contemporary Britain. The film depicts relationships formed in ignorance and fear by the classes which make up the underworld, dependent for its existence on the excremental elements of London low-life. It has been said that the people in the film were examples of the seamy side of London, both Black and White. There can be no equivalence, however, because the multiplicity of Black experiences is constantly avoided by White film-makers. The past and present experiences of the relationship between Black and White means that no Black image can be considered innocent of our complex histories.

Pseudo-scientific definitions of 'race' have informed racist discourse and 'race' has no existence outside of that discourse. Nonetheless, in spite of the misconceptions which inform popular notions of racial difference, the division of peoples into racial groupings has a tenacious currency which has proved difficult to dispel. To further complicate the issue, the matrix of perceptions associated with these notions make it impossible to separate the connotations of the word 'race' from its denotative meaning. The connotations are locked into a system of value-weighted, binary oppositions – Black/White, tainted/pure, dirty/clean, alien/indigenous and so on, from which it is difficult to extricate ourselves. Inequality is enshrined in the concept of racial difference and the relationship between the differences is one of domination and subordination.

Racism does not appear to be simply a phenomenon produced by a single factor such as capitalism, colonialism or just aberrant, prejudiced individuals. It is a construct woven from all these factors and others in various combinations, and the way in which each of the components interact is in a continual state of flux. Racist discourse is not monolithic: it is subject to transformation by various combinations of political, economic or psychological imperatives and it is always multi-faceted. The issue of individual racial prejudice has to be understood as a crucial part of the history of racism, and economic explanations alone are insufficient in this context. Marxism, for instance, has not found an adequate model within which to locate and combat racism: this particular form of oppression is resistant to an inflexible class-based analysis.

Feminism has also failed to make much impact upon the understanding of racism, and even to deal with its pervasiveness in the (White) women's movement. In fact, one of the problems associated with psychoanalytic theory for Black feminists is that its appropriation by White feminists meant that while insights into patriarchal systems were developed, the potential for examining racism in the same moment was not exploited. Women's aspirations as given voice by White feminists did not take cognisance of White women's collusion in racial oppression.

> For purposes of analysis, Black feminists agree that class is as significant as race ... however ... it is clear that Afro-American women have historically formulated identity and political allegiance in terms of race rather than gender or class.[24]

If we suppose that the psychic development of human beings is not biologically pre-determined but that the subject can articulate only that which language within the pre-existing social and symbolic order allows, the White child's experience of the Black is never 'original' as the difference is already invested with meanings ascribed to it by the cultural context into which that child is born. The process of human development is not in itself an inherently negative experience: it is the way in which it is channelled in our existing, inequitable system of social relations that is at fault.

Notes

[1] Frantz Fanon, *The Wretched of the Earth*, London 1967, p160. Although Fanon felt that psychoanalytic theory could be of use to Black people, he was distrustful of the uses to which it might be put: he also noted the absence of consideration of 'race' issues in the work of Freud, Jung and Adler.

[2] Robert M. Young, *Anti-Racist Science Teaching*, London 1987, p16.

[3] See 'Mental Health Services to the Afro-Caribbean Community in West Lambeth: A Survey Report', Afro-Caribbean Mental Health Association 1989, and 'Psychiatry and the Corporate State', Black Health Workers and Patients Group, in *Race and Class*, No.25, Vol.2.

[4] Fanon, *op.cit.*, p151.

[5] During this period there was a resurgence of interest in Fanon's work: in particular the Black Power Movement and other oppressed groups gained valuable insights from *Black Skin, White Masks* and *The Wretched of the Earth*.

[6] Kovel did not consider these types to be definitive in as much as he recognised the shifting nature of bigoted beliefs and that there would inevitably be some overlapping psychological and behavioural features.

[7] Joel Kovel, *White Racism: a Psychohistory*, London 1988 (1970), p61.

[8] Neil Jordan, interviewed in *City Limits*, (4-11 September 1986). See also interview with the two writers in *The Guardian*, (28 August 1986). It is interesting to note in this interview how Leland talks of Simone as if she were someone other than a product of his own (White, middle-class) fantasy.

[9] Kovel, *op.cit.*, p195.

[10] Sander Gilman, *Difference and Pathology: Stereotypes of Sexuality, Race and Madness*, New York 1985, p118.

[11] *Ibid.*, p119.

[12] See Richard Dyer's article 'White', in *Screen*, 'The Last Special Issue on Race?', Vol.29, No.4, Autumn 1988, pp44-64, for case studies of 'Whiteness' in three films and useful introduction to this area of study.

[13] Gilman, *op.cit.*, p17.

[14] *Ibid.*, p25.

[15] It is interesting to apply the 'commutation test' and speculate on how the narrative might have developed had Simone been a White prostitute. See John O. Thompson, 'Screen Acting and the Commutation Test', in *Screen*, Vol.19, No.2, Summer 1978, pp55-70.

[16] Fanon, *op.cit.*, p154-5.

[17] Diana Ross' star vehicle 'Mahogany' (1975) and Eddie Murphy's box-office hit 'Trading Places' (1983) are examples which spring to mind.

[18] This is not referred to in the film but Cathy Tyson's 'mixed race' parentage is mentioned in articles in the *Morning Star* (5 September 1986) and *City Limits* (4-11 September 1986).

[19] Gilman, *op.cit.*, p25.

[20] The complexities of Black people and their positioning as members of cinema audiences are only just beginning to be explored. Of particular relevance to 'Mona Lisa' is Jane Gaines' article 'White Privilege and Looking: Race and Gender in Feminist Film Theory', in *Screen*, Vol.29, No.4, Autumn 1988, pp12-27.

[21] Gilman, *op.cit.*, p20.

[22] See, for example, *Today* (7 September 1986), *Sunday Express* (7 September 1989), *The Guardian* (28 August 1986).

[23] Graham Fuller, in conversation with Neil Jordan and David Leland, *The Guardian* (28 August 1986).

[24] Gaines, *op.cit.*

(For Ben, who would have understood.)

The Third Space

Interview with Homi Bhabha

Homi Bhabha lectures in English and Literary Theory at Sussex University. His writing on colonialism, race, identity and difference have been an important influence on debates in cultural politics. His own essays will be collected into a single volume, *The Location of Culture*, and he is editor of another collection of essays, *Nation and Narration* (both published by Routledge).

Homi Bhabha has played a central role in articulating a response from black intellectuals in Britain to the publication of Salman Rushdie's *The Satanic Verses*. His statement, which emerged from the group 'Black Voices', in *New Statesman & Society* (3 March 1989) argues for a position that refutes both fundamentalism and its liberal response. In the statement he poses the question: 'So where do we turn, we who see the limits of liberalism and fear the absolutist demands of fundamentalism?' The following interview attempts to provide some kind of theoretical chart for that journey.

Jonathan: In your essay 'Commitment to Theory'[1] you analyse the processes of cultural change and transformation. Central to this analysis is your distinction between cultural diversity and cultural difference, and alongside your emphasis on difference are the notions of translation and hybridity. Could you say something about these terms you use?

Homi Bhabha: The attempt to conceive of cultural difference as opposed to cultural diversity comes from an awareness that right through the liberal tradition, particularly in philosophical relativism and in forms of anthropology, the idea that cultures are diverse and that in some sense the diversity of cultures is a good and positive thing and ought to be encouraged, has been known for a long time. It is a commonplace of plural, democratic societies to say that they can encourage and accommodate cultural diversity.

In fact the sign of the 'cultured' or the 'civilised' attitude is the ability to appreciate cultures in a kind of *musée imaginaire*; as though one should be able to collect and appreciate them. Western connoisseurship is the capacity to understand and locate cultures in a universal time-frame that acknowledges their various historical and social contexts only eventually to transcend them and render them transparent.

Following from this, you begin to see the way in which the endorsement of cultural diversity becomes a bedrock of multicultural education policy in this country. There are two problems with it: one is the very obvious one, that although there is always an entertainment and encouragement of cultural diversity, there is always also a corresponding containment of it. A transparent norm is constituted, a norm given by the host society or dominant culture, which says that 'these other cultures are fine, but we must be able to locate them within our own grid'. This is what I mean by a *creation* of cultural diversity and a *containment* of cultural difference.

The second problem is, as we know very well, that in societies where multiculturalism is encouraged racism is still rampant in various forms. This is because the universalism that paradoxically permits diversity masks ethnocentric norms, values and interests.

The changing nature of what we understand as the 'national population' is ever more visibly constructed from a range of different sorts of interests, different kinds of cultural histories, different postcolonial lineages, different sexual orientations. The whole nature of the public sphere is changing so that we really do need the notion of a politics which is based on unequal, uneven, multiple and *potentially antagonistic*, political identities. This must not be confused with some form of autonomous, individualist pluralism (and the corresponding notion of cultural diversity); what is at issue is a historical moment in which these multiple identities do actually articulate in challenging ways, either positively or negatively, either in progressive or regressive ways, often conflictually, sometimes even *incommensurably* – not some flowering of individual talents and capacities. Multiculturalism represented an attempt both to respond to and to control the dynamic process of the articulation of cultural difference, administering a *consensus* based on a norm that propagates cultural diversity.

My purpose in talking about cultural difference rather than cultural diversity is to acknowledge that this kind of liberal relativist perspective is inadequate in itself and doesn't generally recognise the universalist and normative stance from which it constructs its cultural and political judgements. With the concept of difference, which has its theoretical history in post-structuralist thinking, psychoanalysis (where difference is very resonant), post-Althusserian Marxism, and the exemplary work of Fanon, what I was attempting to do was to begin to see how the notion of the West itself, or Western culture, its liberalism and relativism – these very potent mythologies of 'progress' – also contain a cutting edge, a limit. With the notion of cultural difference, I try to place myself in that position of liminality, in that productive space of the construction of culture as difference, in the spirit of alterity or otherness.

The difference of cultures cannot be something that can be accommodated within a universalist framework. Different cultures, the difference between cultural practices, the difference in the construction of cultures within different groups, very often set up among and between themselves an *incommensurability*. However rational you are, or 'rationalist' you are (because rationalism is an ideology, not just a way of being sensible), it is actually very difficult, even impossible and counterproductive, to try and fit together different forms of culture and to pretend that they can easily coexist. The assumption that at some level all forms of cultural diversity may be understood on the basis of a particular universal concept, whether it be 'human being', 'class' or 'race', can be both very dangerous and very limiting in trying to understand the ways in which cultural practices construct their own systems of meaning and social organisation.

Relativism and universalism both have their radical forms, which can be more attractive, but even these are basically part of the same process. At this point I'd like to introduce the notion of 'cultural translation' (and my use of the word is informed by the very original observations of Walter Benjamin on the task of translation and on the task of the translator[2]) to suggest that all forms of culture are in some way related to each other, because culture is a signifying or symbolic activity. The articulation of cultures is possible not because of the familiarity or similarity of *contents*, but because all cultures are symbol-forming and subject-constituting, interpellative practices.

We are very resistant to thinking how the act of signification, the act of producing the icons and symbols, the myths and metaphors through which we live culture, must always – by virtue of the fact that they *are* forms of representation – have within them a kind of self-alienating limit. Meaning is constructed across the bar of difference and separation between the signifier and the signified. So it follows that no culture is full unto itself, no culture is plainly plenitudinous, not only because there are other cultures which contradict its authority, but also because its own symbol-forming activity, its own interpellation in the process of representation, language, signification and meaning-making, always underscores the claim to an originary, holistic, organic identity. By translation I first of all mean a process by which, in order to objectify cultural meaning, there always has to be a process of alienation and of secondariness *in relation to itself*. In that sense there is no 'in itself' and 'for itself' within cultures because they are always subject to intrinsic forms of translation. This theory of culture is close to a theory of language, as part of a process of translations – using that word as before, not in a strict linguistic sense of translation as in a 'book translated from French into English', but as a motif or trope as Benjamin suggests for the activity of displacement within the linguistic sign.

Developing that notion, translation is also a way of imitating, but in a mischevious, displacing sense – imitating an original in such a way that the priority of the original is not reinforced but by the very fact that it *can* be simulated, copied, transferred, transformed, made into a simulacrum and so on: the 'original' is never finished or complete in itself. The 'originary' is always open to translation so that it can never be said to have a totalised prior moment of being or meaning – an essence. What this really means is that cultures are only constituted in relation to that otherness internal to their own symbol-forming activity which makes them decentred structures – through that displacement or liminality opens up the possibility of articulating *different*, even incommensurable cultural practices and priorities.

Now the notion of hybridity comes from the two prior descriptions I've given of the genealogy of difference and the idea of translation, because if, as I was saying, the act of cultural translation (both as representation and as reproduction) denies the essentialism of a prior given original or originary culture, then we see that all forms of culture are continually in a process of hybridity. But for me the importance of hybridity is not to be able to trace two original moments from which the third emerges, rather hybridity to me is the 'third space' which enables other positions to emerge. This third space displaces the histories that constitute it, and sets up new structures of authority, new political initiatives, which are inadequately understood through received wisdom.

Jonathan: I can see how this enables us to elude a politics of polarity and a cultural binarism, but would you call this 'third space' an identity as such?

Homi Bhabha: No, not so much identity as identification (in the psychoanalytic sense). I try to talk about hybridity through a psychoanalytic analogy, so that identification is a process of identifying with and through another object, an object of otherness, at which point the agency of identification – the subject – is itself always ambivalent, because of the intervention of that otherness. But the importance of hybridity is that it bears the traces of those feelings and practices which inform it, just like a translation, so that hybridity puts together the traces of certain other meanings or discourses. It does not give them the authority of being prior in the sense of being original: they are prior only in the sense of being anterior. The process of cultural hybridity gives rise to something different, something new and unrecognisable, a new area of negotiation of meaning and representation. A good example would be the form of hybridity that *The Satanic Verses*[3] represents, where clearly a number of controversies around the origin, the authorship and indeed the authority of the Koran, have been drawn upon in the book.

Within the discourses of theological disputation, what appears in

Identity

Rushdie's *The Satanic Verses* has all been said and discussed before
(about the interpolations in the Koran, the status of those
interpolations, the 'Satanic Verses' as illicit intervention and so on).
What is interesting is how, using another kind of language of
representation – call it the 'migrant metaphor', call it the
postmodern novel or what you will – and giving a context of other
forms of allegorisation, the metropolitanism of the modern city,
contemporary sexuality etc, the knowledges and disputes about the
status of the Koran become quite different things in *The Satanic
Verses*. Through that transformation, through that form of cultural
translation, their values and effects (political, social, cultural)
become entirely incommensurable with the traditions of theological
or historical interpretation which formed the received culture of
Koranic reading and writing.

To think of migration as metaphor suggests that the very language
of the novel, its form and rhetoric, must be open to meanings that
are ambivalent, doubling and dissembling. Metaphor produces
hybrid realities by yoking together unlikely traditions of thought.
The Satanic Verses is, in this sense, structured around the metaphor
of migrancy. The importance of thinking migration as *literary
metaphor* leads us back to the great social offence of the novel (the
way it has been read and interpreted, literally, as a Satanic challenge
to the authority of Islam), but also permits us to see how it is the
form of the novel has been profoundly misunderstood and has
proved to be politically explosive – precisely because the novel is
about metaphor.

Jonathan: Before we talk about *The Satanic Verses*, I'd like to
return the distinction you make between identity and identification.
Could you expand on this?

Homi Bhabha: I felt that the possibility of producing a culture
which both articulates difference and lives with it could only be
established on the basis of a non-sovereign notion of self. It seemed
to me that the way in which left politics deals with that is simply by
replacing the essentialism of the self, the autonomous identity, with
an essentialist cultural and political identity -'class' most often. So
that the 'individualist' subjectivity of the self is decentred if you like,

but only by substituting some other foundational category, such as class. Through the class matrix, other forms of cultural difference have been normalised and homogenised. As we know, class-based politics in this country, however impeccable its socialist or Marxist credentials, has disavowed to a large extent questions and priorities based on race and gender. The fragmentation of identity is often celebrated as a kind of pure anarchic liberalism or voluntarism, but I prefer to see it as a recognition of the importance of the alienation of the self in the construction of forms of solidarity.

It is only by losing the sovereignty of the self that you can gain the freedom of a politics that is open to the non-assimilationist claims of cultural difference. The crucial feature of this new awareness is that it doesn't need to totalise in order to legitimate political action or cultural practice. That is the real issue.

Having said that, there is also always that other mode where a totalisation becomes the basis of any legitimate political or social consciousness, and when that happens then you lose that all-important *articulating world* (and I use the word specifically) of difference.

Jonathan: I want to return to the Rushdie affair in which that kind of totalisation has occurred: far from two counterposing terms being hybridised and transformed into a third, there is that incommen-surability – the sense of two camps, immoveable and locked in a seemingly irreconcilable conflict. Could you comment on this?

Homi Bhabha: As far as the Rushdie case goes, you're quite right to note that at one level what we see is a very intractable, obstinate sort of fixity of difference being established. But you see, just at a practical level, that's not entirely so. At a surface level there is for instance the liberal viewpoint which proposes the right to write, the right to speak, the right to express your beliefs as central to secular society. There has been the firm assertion of those 'fundamentals', but in all quarters which matter there has also been a slow modification of that position. This modification has been to dilute it with comments on the unreadability of the book. I think all this is very interesting: 'of course we have the right to write, but that doesn't mean we like what is written; in fact the more we say we don't like it, the more we both in one or another subtle way send signals to the Iranians that we're dissociating ourselves from it and send signals to our own liberal alter egos that we are such fine people because we are even going to support what we don't like.' Within that liberal wing of the controversy then, there is a very interesting sort of fail-safe strategy which is more complex than saying 'we stick to our liberal values'. In terms of the 'fundamentalist' position (as it is simplistically and wrongly called), you are quite right – even according to the latest opinion poll, 38 per cent of British Muslims think that the death penalty is the correct one for Salman Rushdie.[4] But I think the case has also illustrated how within the Shi'ite sect (which is too easily and too often read as 'fundamentalist') there are a number of other positions. Now it is true that those positions are not dominant at the moment but it has raised – and this is where I think I would make a claim, a practical claim, for a kind of hybridisation which exists no matter whether you keep on asserting the purity of your own doctrines – it has raised more graphically than before the notion of religious law versus secular law, and the presence of a kind of conflictual enunciative moment or enunciative aperture through which, whether you like it or not, your 'fundamentalist' credo is going to have to pass. So it's actually raised a lot of questions about the espousal of contemporary fundamental belief and the world in which 'fundamentalism' has to exist now. It is worth mentioning at this point that Ziauddin Sardar has recently argued in *The Listener* (25 January 1990) that the *fatwah* ['death sentence'] emerges out of that body of classical juridical opinion known as *figh*, which is devoid of the ethical teachings of the Koran 'and many of the laws derived from it are irrelevant for modern *Muslim* societies'.

None of this has directly affected the material situation, but if we try to look at it with a little hindsight, or if we advance our positions a few years and then look back, we'll see how that even within the apparently intractable 'fundamentalist' position, a number of incommensurabilities has emerged (not at the level of theological interpretation, but at the level of effectivity – how these ideas can effected upon a social context and what the social context of these ideas is). So in a rather startling sense, whereas 'fundamentalism' has been so easily relegated to some archaic past, we now begin to see how it is a player in contention in a very modern political game and in fact how many contemporary political moments both make a space for it and limit it. The effective historical context of *The Satanic Verses* conflict is British Bradford, not Shi'ite Iran.

Jonathan: You are arguing then that the problem of modernity has been its inability to deal with archaic cultural forms that it sees as being opposed to itself. What concerns me about all forms of essentialism, and its more conservative cousin – fundamentalism – is that they deny difference and erase their practices of discrimination and domination. Could you comment on this theme? I suppose, for me, the Rushdie affair has brought this up most of all, but so also has the rise of Christian fundamentalism.

Homi Bhabha: Can I just clarify that what to me is problematic about the understanding of the 'fundamentalist' position in the Rushdie case is that it is *represented* as archaic, almost medieval. It may sound very strange to us, it may sound absolutely absurd to some people, but the point is that the demands over *The Satanic Verses* are being made *now*, out of a particular political state that is functioning very much in our time, if not in an immediately recognisable intellectual space. Besides this, many of the Muslims making the demands are not a million miles away, they are not part of another kind of social and cultural world, another society – they happen to live in Bradford. I think that we wilfully misunderstand the issue by relegating them to some distant past from which their voices seem to be emerging in a completely untimely, despotic cry for blood.

Jonathan: In that case, the question of modernity raises a real problem for the left which has always tried to align itself with an idea of progress, linked to that tradition of Western philosophical liberalism which you described and criticised before.

Homi Bhabha: Exactly, it has to keep asserting how modern and how rational it is, and has assumed moreover that these things were identical. But as a critique of the left and its enthusiastic espousal of forms of rationalism and modernity, I think that the question to ask is about the left not being able to cope with certain forms of uncertainty and unfixity in the construction of political identity and its programmatic, policy implications.

Jonathan: But the espousal of essentialism, the insistence that one possesses the truth, demands the fixity of cultural identity. How do your notions of hybridity and difference cope with making alliances with constituencies whose values are, for want of a better word, fundamentalist?

Homi Bhabha: I think very easily, because the notion of hybridity (as I make clear in the piece 'Commitment to Theory' to which you referred earlier) is about the fact that in any particular political struggle, new sites are always being opened up, and if you keep referring those new sites to old principles, then you are not actually able to participate in them fully and productively and creatively. As Nelson Mandela said only the other day, even if there is a war on you must negotiate – negotiation is what politics is all about. And we do negotiate even when we don't know we are negotiating: we are always negotiating in any situation of political opposition or antagonism. Subversion is negotiation; transgression is negotiation; negotiation is not just some kind of compromise or 'selling out' which people too easily understand it to be. Similarly we need to reformulate what we mean by 'reformism': all forms of political activity, especially progressive or radical activity, involve refor-mations and reformulations. With some historical hindsight we may call it 'revolution', those critical moments, but what is actually happening if you slow them up are very fast reforms and reformulations. So I think that political negotiation is a very important issue, and hybridity is precisely about the fact that when a new situation, a new alliance formulates itself, it may demand that you should translate your principles, rethink them, extend them. On the Left there's too much of a timid traditionalism – always trying to read a new situation in terms of some pre-given model or paradigm, which is a reactionary reflex, a conservative 'mindset'.

Jonathan: My earlier question about alliances with fundamentalist constituencies had in mind the topical and attractive idea of a red/green alliance. It seems to me that there is a powerful element within the contemporary explosion of green consciousness that represents a search for fundamental values, for the idea of the sacred – the sanctity of mother earth, the turn away from culture to nature as the font of knowledge.

Homi Bhabha: Now in terms of something like Green politics, I think the situation is very complex, because the great spur to Green politics, however it's coming out now, has been the nuclear threat which was given an eerie prophetic prefiguring in Chernobyl. I think we have not fully assessed the psychological and indeed political effects of something like Chernobyl. With an earthquake you can feel that it's part nature, part culture, whereas with Chernobyl it's entirely culture, entirely science, entirely of our planning and our making. (Not that the disaster is of our planning, but in terms of general perspectives.) The fact that both Chernobyl and Bhopal – those monumental environmental tragedies – are accidents, makes the Green argument even more compelling; we need to look at the history of those accidents. The extent to which Green politics emerges out of such a history and such a critique of rationality and scientific progress is a very good thing. If, as Green politicians are prepared to say, Green politics is not compatible with a capitalist view of social development, to that extent too it's a very good antidote to another prevalent ideology (that Patrick Wright has written about[5]) which informs the English notion of self, and the whole notion of an Arcadian past. You have it in literature with F.R. Leavis; you even have it crawling round the edges of E.P. Thompson sometimes; and you certainly have it in Enoch Powell, where the English countryside becomes inextricably entwined with the Empire, an idea of organic community and so on. It's a very good antidote, because Green politics takes the language of that kind of Arcadianism and turns it against itself. A properly constructed socialist Green Party would naturally provide a critique of the claims of modern, technological-industrial, capitalist development which is ruining the planet; but it would also deconstruct the obfuscatory, nostalgic Arcadianism of the Conservatives.

Jonathan: We've talked about the significance of Green politics and new cultural and religious forces in this country as a challenge to modernity. I'd like to refer to your comment that the founding moment of modernity was the moment of colonialism. In a *Marxism Today* interview[5] you said 'the colonial moment is the history of the West'. Can you elaborate on this remark?

Homi Bhabha: I think we need to draw attention to the fact that the advent of Western modernity, located as it generally is in the 18th and 19th centuries, was the moment when certain master narratives of the state, the citizen, cultural value, art, science, *the novel*, when these major cultural discourses and identities came to define the 'Enlightenment' of Western society and the critical rationality of Western personhood. The time at which these things were happening was the same time at which the West was producing another history of itself through its colonial possessions and relations. That ideological tension, visible in the history of the West as a despotic power, at the very moment of the birth of democracy and modernity, has not been adequately written in a contradictory and contrapuntal discourse of tradition. Unable to resolve that contradiction perhaps, the history of the West as a despotic power, a colonial power, has not been adequately written side by side with its claims to democracy and solidarity. The material legacy of this repressed history is inscribed in the return of post-colonial peoples to the metropolis. Their very presence there changes the politics of the metropolis, its cultural ideologies and its intellectual traditions, because they – as a people who have been recipients of a colonial cultural experience – displace some of the great metropolitan narratives of progress and law and order, and question the authority and authenticity of those narratives. The other point I'm trying to make is not only that the history of colonialism is the history of the West but also that the history of colonialism is a *counter-history* to the normative, traditional history of the West.

The migrant metaphor I discussed before suggests, by analogy, that the Western, metropolitan histories of progress and *civitas* cannot be conceived without evoking the savage colonial antecedents of the ideals of civility and the mythology of 'civilisation'. By implication, it also suggests that the language of rights and obligations, so central to the modern discourse of

218

citizenship, must be questioned on the basis of the anomalous and discriminatory legal and cultural status assigned to migrant and refugee populations who find themselves, inevitably, on the other side of the law.

In other words, the postcolonial perspective forces us to rethink the profound limitations of a consensual and collusive 'liberal' sense of community. It insists – through the migrant metaphor – that cultural and political identity is constructed through a process of othering. The time for 'assimilating' minorities to holistic and organic notions of cultural value has passed – the very language of cultural community needs to be rethought from a postcolonial perspective. A comparison which is 'closer to home' would be the profound shift in the language of sexuality and self effected by feminism in the 1970s, and by the gay community in the 1980s.

Western 'civility' claims, in a world-historical sense, to have superceded all this, maintaining that the perceived cultural values of 'fundamentalism' form part of a past history which is understood, known and located through the aegis and frameworks of Western rationalism and historicism. But the critique mounted by Green politics, and the challenge of radical Islam, flatly contradict that claim – albeit in very different ways.

'Fundamentalist' demands may sound archaic but they are put today as part of a cultural and political system that is fully contemporary. One has to take responsibility for precisely that type of cultural incommensurability and antagonism that my notion of cultural difference attempts to develop.

Jonathan: I'd like to complete this interview with reference to politics, specifically to the role of intellectuals. Can you expand on the comment you made about the place and time of the 'committed intellectual'?

Homi Bhabha: Well, that comment was made in a piece where I was trying to say that committed intellectuals have a dual responsibility.[6] They have a responsibility to intervene in particular struggles, in particular situations of political negotiation, but that is not to say that there is a way of intervening by actually changing the 'object' of knowledge itself, by reformulating the concept of society within which certain demands are made; and I was suggesting that there were therefore two possible forms of activity. I was also attacking a sense that people felt that unless theoretical ideas immediately translated into political action, then they were in some way valueless. Of course the word to focus on here is 'immediately', because very often people say 'well, how does this cash out?'. You articulate a particular theoretical position, the next question will be 'in that case, how do you explain the miners' strike?' or 'how would you explain agitation on London Transport?'. Now I don't believe that this should be a test of the political relevance of a theoretical position, because it may be perfectly possible to suggest two coexistent kinds of activity in which the redefining of larger political concepts is crucial.

Jonathan: This is an intervention in that third space ...

Homi Bhabha: Yes, it's also an intervention in that third space. I mean, for instance, if you just begin to see what's happening in Eastern Europe today – that's a very good example: people are having to redefine not only elements of socialist policy, but also wider questions about the whole nature of this society which is in a process of transition from a communist-state, second-world, iron-curtain frame of being. Socialism in both the East and the West is having to come to terms with the fact that people cannot now be addressed as colossal, undifferentiated collectivities of class, race, gender or nation. The concept of a people is not 'given', as an essential, class-determined, unitary, homogeneous part of society *prior to a politics*; 'the people' are there as a process of political articulation and political negotiation across a whole range of contradictory social sites. 'The people' always exist as a multiple form of identification, waiting to be created and constructed.

This sort of politics, articulating minority constituencies across disjunctive, differential social positions, does not produce that kind of vanguardist 'lead from the front' attitude. If you have this notion of 'the people' as being constructed (through cultural difference and hybridity as I've suggested above), then you avoid that very simplistic polarity between the ruler and the ruled: any monolithic description of authoritative power (such as 'Thatcherism'), based on that kind of binarism, is not going to be a very accurate reflection of what is actually happening in the world. If instead you have a model which emphasises the ambivalent nature of that relationship, which understands political subjectivity as a multi-dimensional, conflictual form of identification, then Thatcherism is the name for a number of articulated constituencies – from working-class and petit-bourgeois formations right up to the expected Tory hierarchies and the commercial/industrial world. You also begin to see how this 'general will', this consensual bloc could be *disarticulated*. What we see is not only political rationality at work, but the 'political unconscious', the symbolic representation of a Great Britain which might in fact be, after a decade of Conservative government, a rather Little country, a modest economic enterprise in Big trouble.

Notes

[1] In *New Formations*, 'Identities' issue, No.5, Summer 1988, Routledge London.
[2] Walter Benjamin, *Illuminations*, Fontana, London 1982.
[3] Salman Rushdie, *The Satanic Verses*, Viking Penguin, London 1988.
[4] Patrick Wright, *On Living in an Old Country: the National Past in Contemporary Britain*, Verso, London 1985.
[5] Discussion with Bhikhu Parekh, in *Marxism Today*, June 1989.
[6] In *New Formations, op.cit.*

Cultural Identity and Diaspora

STUART HALL

A new cinema of the Caribbean is emerging, joining the company of the other 'Third Cinemas'. It is related to, but different from the vibrant film and other forms of visual representation of the Afro-Caribbean (and Asian) 'blacks' of the diasporas of the West – the new post-colonial subjects. All these cultural practices and forms of representation have the black subject at their centre, putting the issue of cultural identity in question. Who is this emergent, new subject of the cinema? From where does he/she speak? Practices of representation always implicate the positions from which we speak or write – the positions of *enunciation*. What recent theories of enunciation suggest is that, though we speak, so to say 'in our own name', of ourselves and from our own experience, nevertheless who speaks, and the subject who is spoken of, are never identical, never exactly in the same place. Identity is not as transparent or unproblematic as we think. Perhaps instead of thinking of identity as an already accomplished fact, which the new cultural practices then represent, we should think, instead, of identity as a 'production', which is never complete, always in process, and always constituted within, not outside, representation. This view problematises the very authority and authenticity to which the term, 'cultural identity', lays claim.

We seek, here, to open a dialogue, an investigation, on the subject of cultural identity and representation. Of course, the 'I' who writes here must also be thought of as, itself, 'enunciated'. We all write and speak from a particular place and time, from a history and a culture which is specific. What we say is always 'in context', *positioned*. I was born into and spent my childhood and adolescence in a lower-middle-class family in Jamaica. I have lived all my adult life in England, in the shadow of the black diaspora – 'in the belly of the beast'. I write against the background of a lifetime's work in cultural studies. If the paper seems preoccupied with the diaspora experience and its narratives of displacement, it is worth remembering that all discourse is 'placed', and the heart has its reasons.

There are at least two different ways of thinking about 'cultural identity'. The first position defines 'cultural identity' in terms of one, shared culture, a sort of collective 'one true self', hiding inside the many other, more superficial or artificially imposed 'selves', which people with a shared history and ancestry hold in common. Within the terms of this definition, our cultural identities reflect the common historical experiences and shared cultural codes which provide us, as 'one people', with stable, unchanging and continuous frames of reference and meaning, beneath the shifting divisions and vicissitudes of our actual history. This 'oneness', underlying all the other, more superficial differences, is the truth, the essence, of 'Caribbean-ness', of the black experience. It is this identity which a Caribbean or black diaspora must discover, excavate, bring to light and express through cinematic representation.

Such a conception of cultural identity played a critical role in all the post-colonial struggles which have so profoundly reshaped our world. It lay at the centre of the vision of the poets of 'Negritude', like Aimée Ceasire and Leopold Senghor, and of the Pan-African political project, earlier in the century. It continues to be a very powerful and creative force in emergent forms of representation amongst hitherto marginalised peoples. In post-colonial societies, the rediscovery of this identity is often the object of what Frantz Fanon once called a

> passionate research ... directed by the secret hope of discovering beyond the misery of today, beyond self-contempt, resignation and abjuration, some very beautiful and splendid era whose existence rehabilitates us both in regard to ourselves and in regard to others.

New forms of cultural practice in these societies address themselves to this project for the very good reason that, as Fanon puts it, in the recent past,

Colonisation is not satisfied merely with holding a people in its grip and emptying the native's brain of all form and content. By a kind of perverted logic, it turns to the past of oppressed people, and distorts, disfigures and destroys it.[1]

The question which Fanon's observation poses is, what is the nature of this 'profound research' which drives the new forms of visual and cinematic representation? Is it only a matter of unearthing that which the colonial experience buried and overlaid, bringing to light the hidden continuities it suppressed? Or is a quite different practice entailed – not the rediscovery but the *production* of identity. Not an identity grounded in the archaeology, but in the *re-telling* of the past?

We should not, for a moment, underestimate or neglect the importance of the act of imaginative rediscovery which this conception of a rediscovered, essential identity entails. 'Hidden histories' have played a critical role in the emergence of many of the most important social movements of our time – feminist, anti-colonial and anti-racist. The photographic work of a generation of Jamaican and Rastafarian artists, or of a visual artist like Armet Francis (a Jamaican-born photographer who has lived in Britain since the age of eight) is a testimony to the continuing creative power of this conception of identity within the emerging practices of representation. Francis's photographs of the peoples of The Black Triangle, taken in Africa, the Caribbean, the USA and the UK, attempt to reconstruct in visual terms 'the underlying unity of the black people whom colonisation and slavery distributed across the African diaspora.' His text is an act of imaginary reunification.

Crucially, such images offer a way of imposing an imaginary coherence on the experience of dispersal and fragmentation, which is the history of all enforced diasporas. They do this by representing or 'figuring' Africa as the mother of these different civilisations. This Triangle is, after all, 'centred' in Africa. Africa is the name of the missing term, the great aporia, which lies at the centre of our cultural identity and gives it a meaning which, until recently, it lacked. No one who looks at these textural images now, in the light of the history of transportation, slavery and migration, can fail to understand how the rift of separation, the 'loss of identity', which has been integral to the Caribbean experience only begins to be healed when these forgotten connections are once more set in place. Such texts restore an imaginary fullness or plentitude, to set against the broken rubric of our past. They are resources of resistance and identity, with which to confront the fragmented and pathological ways in which that experience has been reconstructed within the dominant regimes of cinematic and visual representation of the West.

There is, however, a second, related but different view of cultural identity. This second position recognises that, as well as the many points of similarity, there are also critical points of deep and significant *difference* which constitute 'what we really are'; or rather – since history has intervened – 'what we have become'. We cannot speak for very long, with any exactness, about 'one experience, one identity', without acknowledging its other side – the ruptures and discontinuities which constitute, precisely, the Caribbean's 'uniqueness'. Cultural identity, in this second sense, is a matter of 'becoming' as well as of 'being'. It belongs to the future as much as to the past. It is not something which already exists, transcending place, time, history and culture. Cultural identities come from somewhere, have histories. But, like everything which is historical, they undergo constant transformation. Far from being eternally fixed in some essentialised past, they are subject to the continuous 'play' of history, culture and power. Far from being grounded in a mere 'recovery' of the past, which is waiting to be found, and which, when found, will secure our sense of ourselves into eternity, identities are the names we give to the different ways we are positioned by, and position ourselves within, the narratives of the past.

It is only from this second position that we can properly understand the traumatic character of 'the colonial experience'. The ways in which black people, black experiences, were positioned and subject-ed in the dominant regimes of representation were the effects of a critical exercise of cultural power and normalisation. Not only, in Said's 'Orientalist' sense, were we constructed as different and other within the categories of knowledge of the West by those regimes. They had the power to make us see and experience *ourselves* as 'Other'. Every regime of representation is a regime of

225

power formed, as Foucault reminds us, by the fatal couplet, 'power/knowledge'. But this kind of knowledge is internal, not external. It is one thing to position a subject or set of peoples as the Other of a dominant discourse. It is quite another thing to subject them to that 'knowledge', not only as a matter of imposed will and domination, by the power of inner compulsion and subjective con-formation to the norm. That is the lesson – the sombre majesty – of Fanon's insight into the colonising experience in *Black Skin, White Masks*.

This inner expropriation of cultural identity cripples and deforms. If its silences are not resisted, they produce, in Fanon's vivid phrase, 'individuals without an anchor, without horizon, colourless, stateless, rootless – a race of angels'.[2] Nevertheless, this idea of otherness as an inner compulsion changes our conception of 'cultural identity'. In this perspective, cultural identity is not a fixed essence at all, lying unchanged outside history and culture. It is not some universal and transcendental spirit inside us on which history has made no fundamental mark. It is not once-and-for-all. It is not a fixed origin to which we can make some final and absolute Return. Of course, it is not a mere phantasm either. It is *something* – not a mere trick of the imagination. It has its histories – and histories have their real, material and symbolic effects. The past continues to speak to us. But it no longer addresses us as a simple, factual 'past', since our relation to it, like the child's relation to the mother, is always-already 'after the break'. It is always constructed through memory, fantasy, narrative and myth. Cultural identities are the points of identification, the unstable points of identification or suture, which are made, within the discourses of history and culture. Not an essence but a *positioning*. Hence, there is always a politics of identity, a politics of position, which has no absolute guarantee in an unproblematic, transcendental 'law of origin'.

This second view of cultural identity is much less familiar, and more unsettling. If identity does not proceed, in a straight, unbroken line, from some fixed origin, how are we to understand its formation? We might think of black Caribbean identities as 'framed' by two axes or vectors, simultaneously operative: the vector of similarity and continuity; and the vector of difference and rupture. Caribbean identities always have to be thought of in terms of the dialogic relationship between these two axes. The one gives us some grounding in, some continuity with, the past. The second reminds us that what we share is precisely the experience of a profound discontinuity: the peoples dragged into slavery, transportation, colonisation, migration, came predominantly from Africa – and when that supply ended, it was temporarily refreshed by indentured labour from the Asian subcontinent. (This neglected fact explains why, when you visit Guyana or Trinidad, you see, symbolically inscribed in the faces of their peoples, the paradoxical 'truth' of Christopher Columbus's mistake: you *can* find 'Asia' by sailing west, if you know where to look!) In the history of the modern world, there are few more traumatic ruptures to match these enforced separations from Africa – already figured, in the European imaginary, as 'the Dark Continent'. But the slaves were also from different countries, tribal communities, villages, languages and gods. African religion, which has been so profoundly formative in Caribbean spiritual life, is precisely *different* from Christian monotheism in believing that God is so powerful that he can only be known through a proliferation of spiritual manifestations, present everywhere in the natural and social world. These gods live on, in an underground existence, in the hybridised religious universe of Haitian voodoo, pocomania, Native pentacostalism, Black baptism, Rastafarianism and the black Saints Latin American Catholicism. The paradox is that it was the uprooting of slavery and transportation and the insertion into the plantation economy (as well as the symbolic economy) of the Western world that 'unified' these peoples across their differences, in the same moment as it cut them off from direct access to their past.

Difference, therefore, persists – in and alongside continuity. To return to the Caribbean after any long absence is to experience again the shock of the 'doubleness' of similarity and difference. Visiting the French Caribbean for the first time, I also saw at once how different Martinique is from, say, Jamaica: and this is no mere difference of topography or climate. It is a profound difference of culture and history. And the difference *matters*. It positions Martiniquains and Jamaicans as *both* the same *and* different. Moreover, the boundaries of difference are continually repositioned in relation to different points of reference. Vis-à-vis the developed

West, we are very much 'the same'. We belong to the marginal, the underdeveloped, the periphery, the 'Other'. We are at the outer edge, the 'rim', of the metropolitan world – always 'South' to someone else's *El Norte*.

At the same time, we do not stand in the same relation of the 'otherness' to the metropolitan centres. Each has negotiated its economic, political and cultural dependency differently. And this 'difference', whether we like it or not, is already inscribed in our cultural identities. In turn, it is this negotiation of identity which makes us, vis-à-vis other Latin American people, with a very similar history, different – Caribbeans, *les Antilliennes* ('islanders' to their mainland). And yet, vis-à-vis one another, Jamaican, Haitian, Cuban, Guadeloupean, Barbadian, etc ...

How, then, to describe this play of 'difference' within identity? The common history – transportation, slavery, colonisation – has been profoundly formative. For all these societies, unifying us across our differences. But it does not constitute a common *origin*, since it was, metaphorically as well as literally, a translation. The inscription of difference is also specific and critical. I use the word 'play' because the double meaning of the metaphor is important. It suggests, on the one hand, the instability, the permanent unsettlement, the lack of any final resolution. On the other hand, it reminds us that the place where this 'doubleness' is most powerfully to be heard is 'playing' within the varieties of Caribbean musics. This cultural 'play' could not therefore be represented, cinematically, as a simple, binary opposition – 'past/present', 'them/us'. Its complexity exceeds this binary structure of representation. At different places, times, in relation to different questions, the boundaries are re-sited. They become, not only what they have, at times, certainly been – mutually excluding categories, but also what they sometimes are – differential points along a sliding scale.

One trivial example is the way Martinique both *is* and *is not* 'French'. It is, of course, a *department* of France, and this is reflected in its standard and style of life, Fort de France is a much richer, more 'fashionable' place than Kingston – which is not only visibly poorer, but itself at a point of transition between being 'in fashion' in an Anglo-African and Afro-American way – for those who can afford to be in any sort of fashion at all. Yet, what is distinctively

'Martiniquais' can only be described in terms of that special and peculiar supplement which the black and mulatto skin adds to the 'refinement' and sophistication of a Parisian-derived *haute couture*: that is, a sophistication which, because it is black, is always transgressive.

To capture this sense of difference which is not pure 'otherness', we need to deploy the play on words of a theorist like Jacques Derrida. Derrida uses the anomalous 'a' in his way of writing 'difference' – *differance* – as a marker which sets up a disturbance in our settled understanding or translation of the word/concept. It sets the word in motion to new meanings without erasing the *trace* of its other meanings. His sense of *differance*, as Christopher Norris puts it, thus

> remains suspended between the two French verbs 'to differ' and 'to defer' (postpone), both of which contribute to its textual force but neither of which can fully capture its meaning. Language depends on difference, as Saussure showed ... the structure of distinctive propositions which make up its basic economy. Where Derrida breaks new ground ... is in the extent to which 'differ' shades into 'defer' ... the idea that meaning is always deferred, perhaps to this point of an endless supplementarity, by the play of signification.[3]

This second sense of difference challenges the fixed binaries which stablise meaning and representation and show how meaning is never finished or completed, but keeps on moving to encompass other, additional or supplementary meanings, which, as Norris puts it elsewhere,[4] 'disturb the classical economy of language and representation'. Without relations of difference, no representation could occur. But what is then constituted within representation is always open to being deferred, staggered, serialised.

Where, then, does identity come in to this infinite postponement of meaning? Derrida does not help us as much as he might here, though the notion of the 'trace' goes some way towards it. This is where it sometimes seems as if Derrida has permitted his profound theoretical insights to be reappropriated by his disciples into a celebration of formal 'playfulness', which evacuates them of their political meaning. For if signification depends upon the endless repositioning of its differential terms, meaning, in any specific instance, depends on the contingent and arbitrary stop – the necessary and temporary 'break' in the infinite semiosis of language. This does not detract from the original insight. It only threatens to do so if we mistake this 'cut' of identity – this *positioning*, which makes meaning possible – as a natural and permanent, rather than an arbitrary and contingent 'ending' – whereas I understand every such position as 'strategic' and arbitrary, in the sense that there is no permanent equivalence between the particular sentence we close, and its true meaning, as such. Meaning continues to unfold, so to speak, beyond the arbitrary closure which makes it, at any moment, possible. It is always either over- or under-determined, either an excess or a supplement. There is always something 'left over'.

It is possible, with this conception of 'difference', to rethink the positionings and repositionings of Caribbean cultural identities in relation to at least three 'presences', to borrow Aimée Cesaire's and Leopold Senghor's metaphor: *Présence Africaine, Présence Européenne*, and the third, most ambiguous, presence of all – the sliding term, *Présence Americain*. Of course, I am collapsing, for the moment, the many other cultural 'presences' which constitute the complexity of Caribbean identity (Indian, Chinese, Lebanese etc). I mean America, here, not in its 'first-world' sense – the big cousin to the North whose 'rim' we occupy, but in the second, broader sense: America, the 'New World', *Terra Incognita*.

Présence Africaine is the site of the repressed. Apparently silenced beyond memory by the power of the experience of slavery, Africa was, in fact present everywhere: in the everyday life and customs of the slave quarters, in the languages and patois of the plantations, in names and words, often disconnected from their taxonomies, in the secret syntactical structures through which other languages were spoken, in the stories and tales told to children, in religious practices and beliefs, in the spiritual life, the arts, crafts, musics and rhythms of slave and post-emancipation society. Africa, the signified which could not be represented directly in slavery, remained and remains the unspoken, unspeakable 'presence' in Caribbean culture. It is 'hiding' behind every verbal inflection, every narrative twist of Caribbean cultural life. It is the secret code with which every Western text was 're-read'. It is the ground-bass of every rhythm and bodily movement. *This* was – is – the 'Africa' that 'is alive and well in the diaspora'.[5]

Cultural Identity and Diaspora

When I was growing up in the 1940s and 1950s as a child in Kingston, I was surrounded by the signs, music and rhythms of this Africa of the diaspora, which only existed as a result of a long and discontinuous series of transformations. But, although almost everyone around me was some shade of brown or black (Africa 'speaks'!), I never once heard a single person refer to themselves or to others as, in some way, or as having been at some time in the past, 'African'. It was only in the 1970s that this Afro-Caribbean identity became historically available to the great majority of Jamaican people, at home and abroad. In this historic moment, Jamaicans discovered themselves to be 'black' – just as, in the same moment, they discovered themselves to be the sons and daughters of 'slavery'.

This profound cultural discovery, however, was not, and could not be, made directly, without 'mediation'. It could only be made *through* the impact on popular life of the post-colonial revolution, the civil rights struggles, the culture of Rastafarianism and the music of reggae – the metaphors, the figures or signifiers of a new construction of 'Jamaican-ness'. These signified a 'new' Africa of the New World, grounded in an 'old' Africa: – a spiritual journey of discovery that led, in the Caribbean, to an indigenous cultural revolution; this is Africa, as we might say, necessarily 'deferred' – as a spiritual, cultural and political metaphor.

It is the presence/absence of Africa, in this form, which has made it the privileged signifier of new conceptions of Caribbean identity. Everyone in the Caribbean, of whatever ethnic background, must sooner or later come to terms with this African presence. Black, brown, mulatto, white – all must look *Présence Africaine* in the face, speak its name. But whether it is, in this sense, an *origin* of our identities, unchanged by four hundred years of displacement, dismemberment, transportation, to which we could in any final or literal sense return, is more open to doubt. The original 'Africa' is no longer there. It too has been transformed. History is, in that sense, irreversible. We must not collude with the West which, precisely, normalises and appropriates Africa by freezing it into some timeless zone of the primitive, unchanging past. Africa must at last be reckoned with by Caribbean people, but it cannot in any simple sense by merely recovered.

It belongs irrevocably, for us, to what Edward Said once called an 'imaginative geography and history', which helps 'the mind to intensify its own sense of itself by dramatising the difference between what is close to it and what is far away'. It 'has acquired an imaginative or figurative value we can name and feel'.[7] Our belongingness to it constitutes what Benedict Anderson calls 'an imagined community'.[8] To *this* 'Africa', which is a necessary part of the Caribbean imaginary, we can't literally go home again.

The character of this displaced 'homeward' journey – its length and complexity – comes across vividly, in a variety of texts. Tony Sewell's documentary archival photographs, Garvey's Children: the Legacy of Marcus Garvey, tells the story of a 'return' to an African identity which went, necessarily, by the long route-through London and the United States. It 'ends', not in Ethiopia but with Garvey's statue in front of the St Ann Parish Library in Jamaica: not with a traditional tribal chant but with the music of Burning Spear and Bob Marley's Redemption Song. This is our 'long journey' home. Derek Bishton's courageous visual and written text, *Black Heart Man* – the story of the journey of a *white* photographer 'on the trail of the promised land' – starts in England, and goes, through Shashemene, the place in Ethiopia to which many Jamaican people have found their way on their search for the Promised Land, and slavery; but it ends in Pinnacle, Jamaica, where the first Rastafarian settlements was established, and 'beyond' – among the dispossessed of 20th-century Kingston and the streets of Handsworth, where Bishton's voyage of discovery first began. These symbolic journies are necessary for us all – and necessarily circular. This is the Africa we must return to – but 'by another route': what Africa has *become* in the New World, what we have made of 'Africa': 'Africa' – as we re-tell it through politics, memory and desire.

What of the second, troubling, term in the identity equation – the European presence? For many of us, this is a matter not of too little but of too much. Where Africa was a case of the unspoken, Europe was a case of that which is endlessly speaking – and endlessly speaking *us*. The European presence interrupts the innocence of the whole discourse of 'difference' in the Caribbean by introducing the question of power. 'Europe' belongs irrevocably to the 'play' of power, to the lines of force and consent, to the role of the *dominant*, in Caribbean culture. In terms of colonialism, underdevelopment, poverty and the racism of colour, the European presence is that which, in visual representation, has positioned the black subject within its dominant regimes of representation: the colonial discourse, the literatures of adventure and exploration, the romance of the exotic, the ethnographic and travelling eye, the tropical languages of tourism, travel brochure and Hollywood and the violent, pornographic languages of *ganja* and urban violence.

Because *Présence Européenne* is about exclusion, imposition and expropriation, we are often tempted to locate that power as wholly external to us – an extrinsic force, whose influence can be thrown off like the serpent sheds its skin. What Frantz Fanon reminds us, in *Black Skin, White Masks*, is how this power has become a constitutive element in our own identities.

> The movements, the attitudes, the glances of the other fixed me there, in the sense in which a chemical solution is fixed by a dye. I was indignant; I demanded an explanation. Nothing happened. I burst apart. Now the fragments have been put together again by another self.[9]

This 'look', from – so to speak – the place of the Other, fixes us, not only in its violence, hostility and aggression, but in the ambivalence of its desire. This brings us face to face, not simply with the dominating European presence as the site or 'scene' of integration where those other presences which it had actively disaggregated were recomposed – re-framed, put together in a new way; but as the site of a profound splitting and doubling – what Homi Bhaba has called 'the ambivalent identifications of the racist world ... the 'otherness' of the self inscribed in the perverse palimpsest of colonial identity.'[10]

The dialogue of power and resistance, of refusal and recognition, with and against *Présence Européenne* is almost as complex as the 'dialogue' with Africa. In terms of popular cultural life, it is nowhere to be found in its pure, pristine state. It is always-already fused, syncretised, with other cultural elements. It is always-already creolised – not lost beyond the Middle Passage, but ever-present: from the harmonics in our musics to the ground-bass of Africa, traversing and intersecting our lives at every point. How can we stage this dialogue so that, finally, we can place it, without terror or violence, rather than being forever placed by it? Can we ever recognise its irreversible influence, whilst resisting its imperialising eye? The engima is impossible, so far, to resolve. It requires the most complex of cultural strategies. Think, for example, of the dialogue of every Caribbean filmmaker or writer, one way or another, with the dominant cinemas and literature of the West – the complex relationship of young black British filmmakers with the 'avant-gardes' of European and American filmmaking. Who could describe this tense and tortured dialogue as a 'one way trip'?

The Third, 'New World' presence, is not so much power, as ground, place, territory. It is the juncture-point where the many cultural tributaries meet, the 'empty' land (the European colonisers emptied it) where strangers from every other part of the globe collided. None of the people who now occupy the islands – black, brown, white, African, European, American, Spanish, French, East Indian, Chinese, Portugese, Jew, Dutch – originally 'belonged' there. It is the space where the creolisations and assimilations and syncretisms were negotiated. The New World is the third term – the primal scene – where the fateful/fatal encounter was staged between Africa and the West. It also has to be understood as the place of many, continuous displacements: of the original pre-Columbian inhabitants, the Arawaks, Caribs and Amerindians, permanently displaced from their homelands and decimated; of other peoples displaced in different ways from Africa, Asia and Europe; the displacements of slavery, colonisation and conquest. It stands for the endless ways in which Caribbean people have been destined to 'migrate'; it is the signifier of migration itself – of travelling, voyaging and return as fate, as destiny; of the Antillean as the prototype of the modern or postmodern New World nomad, continually moving between centre and periphery. This preoccupation with movement and migration Caribbean cinema shares with many other 'Third Cinemas', but it is one of our defining themes, and it is destined to cross the narrative of every film script or cinematic image.

Présence Americaine continues to have its silences, its suppressions. Peter Hulme, in his essay on 'Islands of Enchantment'[11] reminds us that the word 'Jamaica' is the Hispanic form of the indigenous Arawak name – 'land of wood and water' – which Columbus's re-naming ('Santiago') never replaced. The Arawak presence remains today a ghostly one, visible in the islands mainly in museums and archeological sites, part of the barely knowable or usable 'past'. Hulme notes that it is not represented in the emblem of the Jamaican National Heritage Trust, for example, which chose instead the figure of Diego Pimienta, 'an African who fought for his Spanish masters against the English invasion of the island in 1655' – a deferred, metonymic, sly and sliding representation of Jamaican identity if ever there was one! He recounts the story of how Prime Minister Edward Seaga tried to alter the Jamaican coat-of-arms, which consists of two Arawak figures holding a shield with five pineapples, surmounted by an alligator. 'Can the crushed and extinct Arawaks represent the dauntless character of Jamaicans? Does the low-slung, near extinct crocodile, a cold-blooded reptile, symbolise the warm, soaring spirit of Jamaicans?' Prime Minister Seaga asked rhetorically.[12] There can be few political statements which so eloquently testify to the complexities entailed in the process of trying to represent a diverse people with a diverse history through a single, hegemonic 'identity'. Fortunately, Mr Seaga's invitation to the Jamaican people, who are overwhelmingly of African descent, to start their 'remembering' by first 'forgetting' something else, got the comeuppance it so richly deserved.

The 'New World' presence – America, *Terra Incognita* – is therefore itself the beginning of diaspora, of diversity, of hybridity and difference, what makes Afro-Caribbean people already people of a diaspora. I use this term here metaphorically, not literally: diaspora does not refer us to those scattered tribes whose identity can only be secured in relation to some sacred homeland to which they must at all costs return, even if it means pushing other people into the sea. This is the old, the imperialising, the hegemonising, form of 'ethnicity'. We have seen the fate of the people of Palestine at the hands of this backward-looking conception of diaspora – and the complicity of the West with it. The diaspora experience as I intend it here is defined, not by essence or purity, but by the recognition of a necessary heterogeneity and diversity; by a conception of 'identity' which lives with and through, not despite, difference; by *hybridity*. Diaspora identities are those which are constantly producing and reproducing themselves anew, through transformation and difference. One can only think here of what is uniquely – 'essentially' – Caribbean: precisely the mixes of colour, pigmentation, physiognomic type; the 'blends' of tastes that is Caribbean cuisine; the aesthetics of the 'cross-overs', of 'cut-and-mix', to borrow Dick Hebdige's telling phrase, which is the heart and soul of black music. Young black cultural practitioners and critics in Britain are increasingly coming to acknowledge and explore in their work this 'diaspora aesthetic' and its formations in the post-colonial experience:

> Across a whole range of cultural forms there is a 'syncretic' dynamic which critically appropriates elements from the master-codes of the dominant culture and 'creolises' them, disarticulating given signs and re-articulating their symbolic meaning. The subversive force of this hybridising tendency is most apparent at the level of language itself where creoles, patois and black English decentre, destabilise and carnivalise the linguistic domination of 'English' – the nation-language of master-discourse – through strategic inflections, re-accentuations and other performative moves in semantic, syntactic and lexical codes.[13]

It is because this New World is constituted for us as place, a narrative of displacement, that it gives rise so profoundly to a certain imaginary plenitude, recreating the endless desire to return to 'lost origins', to be one again with the mother, to go back to the beginning. Who can ever forget, when once seen rising up out of that blue-green Caribbean, those islands of enchantment. Who has not known, at this moment, the surge of an overwhelming nostalgia for lost origins, for 'times past'? And yet, this 'return to the beginning' is like the imaginary in Lacan – it can neither be fulfilled nor requited, and hence is the beginning of the symbolic, of representation, the infinitely renewable source of desire, memory, myth, search, discovery – in short, the reservoir of our cinematic narratives.

We have been trying, in a series of metaphors, to put in play a different sense of our relationship to the past, and thus a different way of thinking about cultural identity, which might constitute new points of recognition in the discourses of the emerging Caribbean cinema and black British cinemas. We have been trying to theorise identity as constituted, not outside but within representation; and hence of cinema, not as a second-order mirror held up to reflect what already exists, but as that form of representation which is able to constitute us as new kinds of subjects, and thereby enable us to discover places from which to speak. Communities, Benedict Anderson argues in *Imagined Communities* are to be distinguished, not by their falsity/genuineness, but by the style in which they are imagined.[14] This is the vocation of modern black cinemas: by allowing us to see and recognise the different parts and histories of ourselves, to construct those points of identification, those positionalities we call in retrospect our 'cultural identities'.

We must not therefore be content with delving into the past of a people in order to find coherent elements which will counteract colonialism's attempts to falsify and harm ... A national culture is not a folk-lore, nor an abstract populism that believes it can discover a people's true nature. A national culture is the whole body of efforts made by a people in the sphere of thought to describe, justify and praise the action through which that people has created itself and keeps itself in existence.[15]

Notes

[1] Frantz Fanon, 'On National Culture', in *The Wretched of the Earth*, London 1963, p170.
[2] *Ibid.*, p176.
[3] Christopher Norris, *Deconstruction: Theory and Practice*, London 1982, p32.
[4] Christopher Norris, *Jacques Derrida*, London 1987, p15.
[5] Stuart Hall, *Resistance Through Rituals*, London 1976.
[6] Edward Said, *Orientalism*, London 1985, p55.
[7] *Ibid.*
[8] Benedict Anderson, *Imagined Communities: Reflections on the Origin and Rise of Nationalism*, London 1982.
[9] Frantz Fanon, *Black Skin, White Masks*, London 1986, p109.
[10] Homi Bhabha, 'Foreword' to Fanon, *ibid.*, xv.
[11] In *New Formations*, no.3, Winter 1987.
[12] *Jamaica Hansard*, vol.9, 1983-4, p363. Quoted in Hulme, *ibid.*
[13] Kobena Mercer, 'Diaspora Culture and the Dialogic Imagination', in M. Cham and C. Watkins (eds), *Blackframes: Critical Perspectives on Black Independent Cinema*, 1988, p57.
[14] Anderson, *op.cit.*, p15.
[15] Fanon, *op.cit.*, 1963, p188.

This piece was first published in the journal *Framework* (no.36) and is reproduced by kind permission of the editor, Jim Pines.

Biographical Notes

Frances Angela lives in North London.

Zarina Bhimji lives in London and is a practising photo-artist. She works in adult education and is artist-in-residence at Culloden School, assigned there by the Whitechapel Art Gallery. She won the Coopers and Lybrand Award for the most outstanding artist under thirty in the 1989 Whitechapel Art Gallery Open Exhibition.

Homi Bhabha lectures in English and Literary Theory at Sussex University. His writings on colonialism, race, identity and difference are to be published as *Locations of Culture*, he is also editor of another collection of essays, *Nation and Narration*. Both will be published by Routledge.

Stuart Hall is Professor of Sociology at the Open University. He has written extensively on politics, race and culture; a number of these writings have been collected as *The Hard Road to Renewal*, published by Verso. He is also co-editor of *New Times*, published by Lawrence & Wishart.

Kobena Mercer works at the British Film Institute. He has written and lectured widely on film, media and cultural studies and is currently completing research at Goldsmith's College on Enoch Powell's speeches in the 1960s.

Pratibha Parmar is a writer, filmmaker and political activist. She has contributed to and co-edited several books, including 'Many Voices,

One Chant: Black Feminist Perspectives', *Feminist Review*, No. 17 (1984), *Through the Break: Women in Personal Struggle*, Sheba (1987), *Charting the Journey: Writings by Black and Third World Women*, Sheba (1988), *Sari Red* (1988); and her films include *Memory Pictures* and *Flesh and Paper* (Channel Four, 1990). She has also written for *Marxism Today*, *City Limits*, *Spare Rib* and *Ten:8*.

Jonathan Rutherford is co-editor of *Male Order: Unwrapping Masculinity*, Lawrence & Wishart (1988). He is currently working on a PhD on 'Men, Heterosexuality and Difference' at Middlesex Polytechnic.

Andrea Stuart, formerly deputy features editor on *The Voice*, was a contributor to *The Female Gaze*, edited by Lorraine Gammon and Margaret Marshment, The Women's Press (1988).

Simon Watney is a director of the National AIDS Manual. He chairs the Health Education Group of the Terrence Higgins Trust, Britain's oldest and largest non-governmental AIDS service organisation. His most recent book is *Taking Liberties: AIDS and Cultural Politics*, Serpents Tail (1989), which he co-edited with Erica Carter.

Jeffrey Weeks is the author of several books on the history of sexuality and is currently writing a book on values.

Lola Young is the enterprise officer at Middlesex Polytechnic. She is involved in a wide variety of cultural development work relating to black and ethnic arts, and is currently researching cultural theory and race.

CPSIA information can be obtained
at www.ICGtesting.com
Printed in the USA
BVHW042039190719
553750BV00025B/55/P

9 780853 158714